DEC - - 2000

The
American Revolution

The American Revolution

Michael Weber

RAINTREE
STECK-VAUGHN
PUBLISHERS

A Harcourt Company

Austin · New York
www.steck-vaughn.com

Published by Raintree Steck-Vaughn Publishers, an imprint of Steck-Vaughn Company

Developed by Discovery Books
Editor: Sabrina Crewe
Designer: Sabine Beaupré
Maps: Stefan Chabluk

Raintree Steck-Vaughn Publishers Staff
Publishing Director: Walter Kossmann
Project Manager: Joyce Spicer
Editor: Shirley Shalit
Electronic Production: Scott Melcer

Consultant Andrew Frank, California State University, Los Angeles

Library of Congress Cataloging-in-Publication Data
Weber, Michael, 1945-
    The American Revolution / Michael Weber.
       p.   cm. -- (The making of America)
    Includes bibliographical references (p.   ) and index.
    Summary: Traces the history of the American Revolution, from the Boston Massacre to the British surrender at Yorktown.
    ISBN: 0–8172–5702–0
       1. United States — History — Revolution, 1775-1783 — Juvenile literature.
    [1. United States — History — Revolution, 1775-1783.]   I. Title. II. Making of America (Austin, Tex.)
    E208.W36 2000
    973.3—dc 21
                                                    99–055985
Printed and bound in the United States of America
1 2 3 4 5 6 7 8 9 0 IP 04 03 02 01 00 99

Acknowledgments
Cover Corbis; p. 9 The Granger Collection; pp. 10, 11, 12, 14, 17, 18, 21 Corbis; p. 24 The Granger Collection; pp. 25, 27, 30, 31 Corbis; pp. 32, 33 The Granger Collection; pp. 36, 37, 39, 41, 42, 43, 46, 47, 49, 50, 53, 55 Corbis; p. 58 The Granger Collection; pp. 59, 61, 63, 64 Corbis; p. 66 The Granger Collection; pp. 69, 72, 73 Corbis; p. 77 The Granger Collection; p. 81 Corbis; pp. 82, 85 The Granger Collection.

Cover illustration: This painting by Alonzo Chappel shows an event, which took place at Lexington, Massachusetts, on April 19, 1775. that led to the American Revolution.

Contents

Introduction

British-Americans were celebrating in the spring of 1763. Bells rang throughout the British colonies in North America. People lit bonfires, fired cannons, and set off fireworks. They paraded in the streets and made toasts to the British king, George III. After seven years of war, Britain and France had signed a peace treaty in Paris on February 10. The news arrived after several weeks by ship from Europe, and the colonists rejoiced.

The treaty was a triumph for Britain. It ended a war that had been fought in many parts of the world. In North America, the conflict had been called the French and Indian War. Britain and France had battled for control of the eastern part of the continent, and Britain had won. The original inhabitants of America, the Indian peoples, had mostly sided with France. The French seemed much less of a threat to the Indians than Britain's American colonists, with their endless hunger for Indian land.

Under the treaty, France had to hand over to Britain nearly all its territory in North America. Britain already had 13 colonies along the Atlantic Ocean, as well as colonies in Canada and the West Indies. Now it gained the vast area between the Appalachian Mountains and the Mississippi River, and all of Canada. Florida, which had been part of Spain's territories, also went to the British.

Britain's 13 North American colonies extended from Maine (at that time a part of Massachusetts) in the north to Georgia in the south. In 1763, about 500,000 Native Americans lived in the area. Another 2,500,000 people were also living in the colonies. Nearly all of them were white settlers from Europe, but there were about 400,000 black people, most of whom were slaves. The most populated colony was Virginia, with almost 450,000 people. Georgia had the lowest population, with 23,000 people.

The British-American colonists proudly thought of themselves as British citizens. They had helped pay for the French and Indian War with their taxes. Thousands of colonists had served as soldiers, including a young Virginian, Colonel George Washington. Few Americans imagined that the great victory in the war would lead to trouble between America and Britain. But trouble quickly developed, which led to another war and then to the creation of a new nation.

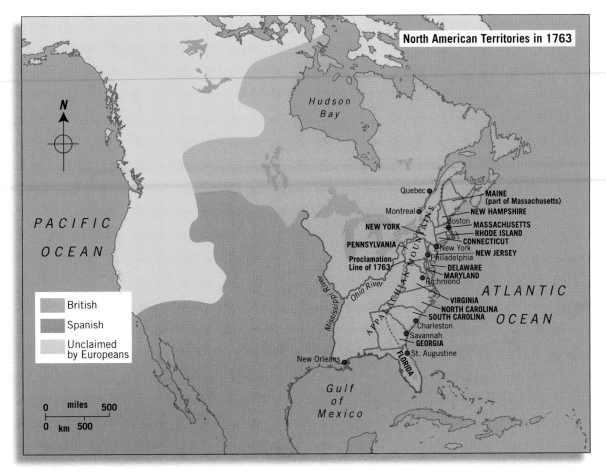

North American Territories in 1763

This map of North America shows British and other European territories after 1763, when France gave up its claims to huge areas of land.

The Road to Conflict

I n Britain, people also celebrated their victory over France. But British leaders soon realized that their much enlarged empire presented them with serious problems.

For many years, Britain had left the American colonists more or less alone. "Salutary neglect" was what one member of Parliament called the British policy. He meant that it was a kind of neglect that was good for America. The British government did control foreign affairs and overseas trade for the colonies. But the colonists pretty much governed themselves as far as their internal affairs were concerned. Their legislatures made laws for them. Taxes were collected and spent as and when they were needed.

The British Change Their Policy

Now this began to change. The problems facing the British led them to adopt new policies toward America.

Native Americans presented the most immediate problem. Now that the French were out of the picture, the Indians feared even more for their lands. In 1763, tribes led by the Ottawa chief Pontiac attacked white settlements along the western frontier of the colonies. The Indians were defeated, but the British government decided to station 10,000 troops in forts along the frontier. This frontier stretched the length of the Appalachian Mountains (see map on page 7). To help keep the peace, King George III made a proclamation in 1763: No colonists could cross the Appalachian Mountains and settle in Indian lands without special permission.

Keeping British soldiers along the frontier was expensive. Moreover, the long war with France had left the British government deeply in debt. In fact, money was the biggest problem facing the British after 1763. They decided they needed more from their American colonies. The British felt the colonists could and should pay higher taxes to the British treasury for the defense and government of the colonies. Americans paid less tax than people in Britain, and not all the taxes Americans owed were collected anyway.

In 1764, the British Parliament passed a series of measures concerning the colonies. One law, the Quartering Act, required colonists to house and feed British troops. Other new laws were designed to tighten British control over the colonies' trade. The laws also raised money through new and higher taxes.

The Sugar Act stopped the colonists from importing goods from anywhere except Britain. It increased taxes on imports and put new taxes on goods like sugar and coffee. This caused people to bring goods into the colonies secretly, by smuggling, so that they could avoid paying the taxes. The British prime minister, George Grenville, set up new courts to try and stop smuggling. These courts didn't give people

Ottawa Indians led by Chief Pontiac lay siege to Fort Detroit, a British settlement on the western frontier in what is now Michigan. The siege lasted for six months before Pontiac withdrew.

King George III (1738–1820)

George III became king of Great Britain and Ireland in 1760 when his grandfather, King George II, died. George III was a very popular king at first, both in Britain and America. He was determined to be a strong ruler, fully in control of his government and the British Parliament. Wanting to reduce the taxes on the British people, George III fully supported making the American colonists pay more. He never understood why the Americans were against new taxes. George III thought of the colonists as rebels, and his attitude made their struggle for independence long and hard. In 1783, the king was forced to grant Americans their independence to end the seven-year Revolutionary War.

George III suffered from porphyria, a rare, inherited disease that causes periods of insanity. He became permanently insane in 1811 and went blind and deaf shortly before his death in 1820.

any of their usual rights, like trial by jury. New regulations also allowed officials to search warehouses, ships, stores, and even homes for goods they suspected might be smuggled. To do this, they used documents called "writs of assistance."

In 1765, Parliament passed another tax law, the Stamp Act. Grenville announced the new measure was needed to cover "the necessary expenses of defending" the colonies. The Stamp Act required colonists to buy a stamp that had to be put on all kinds of printed materials. These included wills, newspapers, books, calendars, even playing cards. The money spent on buying the stamp went straight to the government as another tax. This was the first direct tax on the colonists.

Americans Respond to the Taxes

The new British policies surprised and angered many Americans. The colonists felt they were already paying all they could for their defense. Thousands of them had fought in the French and Indian War, and they felt they had suffered enough.

King George's Proclamation of 1763, regarding Indian land, was deeply resented. Unclaimed land was becoming scarce in the colonies along the Atlantic Coast. From the days of the earliest European settlements, white colonists had come to America to realize their dream of acquiring land. Now the British king seemed to be destroying that dream. And some Americans (including George Washington) had bought land west of the Appalachians, hoping to sell it someday and make a lot of money.

The colonists were used to their taxes being spent on the American colonies. Now they had to pay taxes to provide money for the British treasury. The new sugar and stamp taxes immediately affected people where it hurt: in their wallets. Farmers, innkeepers, students, lawyers, clergymen, merchants—everyone found their expenses increased.

But there was another issue at stake besides money. The colonists thought of themselves as British citizens, with all the rights of people living in Britain. These rights had been won during years of struggle and bloodshed in Britain. The result was a set of traditions and laws that protected citizens against unjust governments.

One of these rights was trial by jury, so that a person accused of wrongdoing could get a fair hearing. Another was the right to be safe and secure in one's own home. But the new courts and the writs of assistance ignored those rights.

"Our houses and even our bedchambers are exposed to be ransacked, our boxes, trunks, and chests broke open, ravaged and plundered by wretches whom no prudent man would venture to employ."

A Bostonian describing the effects of the writs of assistance, 1764

This issue of the Pennsylvania Journal *was filled with cartoons and articles opposing the Stamp Act. On the front page, the publisher says he will stop printing the newspaper until a way can be found to "elude the chains" of the stamp tax.*

One of the most precious rights was the principle of "no taxation without representation." The colonists were paying taxes to Britain, but they were not represented in the British Parliament. So Americans thought that Parliament had no right to tax them. Some influential men in the colonies, many of them lawyers, began to think that the British government was depriving Americans of traditional British liberties.

Many thinkers and leaders in Britain's American colonies believed in a movement of the time called the Enlightenment. Enlightenment thinkers considered life, liberty, and the opportunity to acquire property the natural birthright of all people. They believed that governments were created to protect those basic rights.

Patrick Henry was the greatest speaker of the American Revolution. In 1765 he made a famous speech in the Virginia Assembly, comparing King George III to tyrants of the past.

The Protests Grow

All over the colonies, Americans protested the new taxes and laws. James Otis, a Massachusetts lawyer, published a stirring pamphlet denouncing the Sugar Act. One of the first people to organize protest meetings was Samuel Adams, who later became governor of Massachusetts. At a town meeting in Boston in May 1764, he proposed a resolution saying that Parliament had not acted legally. The Massachusetts Assembly approved the resolution and invited other colonial assemblies to do the same. The assemblies of Connecticut, New York, Pennsylvania, Virginia, and South Carolina did just that.

A year later, a fiery 29-year-old named Patrick Henry introduced protest resolutions in the Virginia Assembly. He defended the colonists' rights as British citizens.

Protests against the new taxes became violent in many places. In New York City, all the stamps were seized by the City Council to prevent the stamp tax from being paid. There were riots in Rhode Island, Maryland, New Jersey, Pennsylvania, Connecticut, and New Hampshire. In several cities, groups of men called Sons of Liberty marched through the streets denouncing the Stamp Act. Sometimes they threatened tax collectors and other British officials with violence. Some British officials were forced to resign.

Young men in port cities like New York had good reason to be hostile to the British. To obtain sailors for their many ships, the Royal Navy seized men from American merchant ships. Sometimes, naval officers would even seize men in the streets. This practice, known as impressment, poisoned relations between Britain and America for many years.

A movement spread through the colonies to boycott, or refuse to buy, British goods. Women's groups called Daughters of Liberty promised to wear only colonial-made dresses. Starting in Rhode Island and then spreading to other colonies, they began to weave cloth to replace British textiles. Towns competed for the honor of having made the most cloth.

Opposition to the stamp tax was so widespread that the British found they could not collect it. Meanwhile, the Massachusetts Assembly had invited all the colonies to send delegates to a meeting to discuss the situation. Nine colonies accepted (New Hampshire, Georgia, North Carolina, and Virginia did not attend) and the Stamp Act Congress met in New York in October 1765. The Congress pledged loyalty to the king but condemned the new taxes. It asked the king and Parliament to repeal them.

"It is inseparable to the freedom of a people, and the undoubted right of Englishmen, that no taxes should be imposed upon them, but with their own consent, given personally, or by their representatives."

Stamp Act Congress, 1765

One way the Sons of Liberty punished the stamp tax collectors was by tarring and feathering. This was a gruesome punishment: The victim would be covered with hot tar and then feathers were stuck all over him. The tar could be removed with grease, but victims took weeks to recover.

New British Laws

British leaders were stunned by the American protests. A bitter debate took place in Parliament. Some members warned against provoking the colonists any further. In March 1766, less than a year after passing the Stamp Act, Parliament repealed it. But the repeal was accompanied by a new law, the Declaratory Act. This act declared that Parliament still had power over the colonies.

Most Americans took no notice of the Declaratory Act. They rejoiced over the repeal of the Stamp Act. Celebrations were held once again. But more trouble lay ahead.

Britain still wanted to raise more money. A new finance minister, Charles Townshend, thought he could obtain money from the colonies without causing the uproar that the Stamp Act did. In this he was sadly mistaken.

In June 1767, Townshend persuaded Parliament to pass a new set of laws, known as the Townshend Acts. New taxes were imposed, but this time on products imported from

Britain. These were essential goods like glass, tea, paper, and lead. They were things that the colonists had to import because they were not made in the colonies.

Some of the money to be raised was to be used to pay the salaries of the British governors and other officials in America. Up to that time, these officials had been paid by the local assemblies, and the colonists did not like the change. They wanted to keep control over money spent by the government. This control was another of their rights as British citizens.

To make things even worse, the Townshend Acts continued the writs of assistance, allowing people's homes to be entered and searched. The Acts even added to the numbers of the courts without juries that were so unpopular. The angry colonists refused once again to buy British goods. This time the boycotts were even more effective.

The crisis worsened when the British government ordered several governors to break up their colonial assemblies. New York's Assembly was dissolved for violating the Quartering Act. The Massachusetts Assembly was dissolved for sending a letter, written by Samuel Adams, to the other colonies urging them to defend their rights. When the Virginia Assembly passed new resolutions asserting American rights, it too was dissolved. Twenty-eight members, including Patrick Henry, George Washington, and Thomas Jefferson, continued to meet in a Williamsburg tavern.

The Sons of Liberty took to the streets again. Customs agents and other British officials in New York and Boston were threatened with violence. The situation grew even worse in the summer of 1768, when customs agents seized a ship on suspicion of smuggling. The ship belonged to John Hancock, a wealthy merchant who had been active in the protests. The royal governor of Massachusetts became very worried about what would happen, and asked for more British troops. They were needed, he said, "to rescue the Government from the hands of a trained mob and to restore the activity of the Civil power."

"COME join Hand in Hand, brave AMERICANS all,

And rouse your bold Hearts at fair LIBERTY'S Call;

No tyrannous Acts shall suppress your just Claim,

Or stain with Dishonour AMERICA's Name–

In freedom we're born and in freedom we'll live,

Our right arms are ready,

Steady, men, steady,

Not as slaves but as freemen, our lives we will give."

John Dickinson, "Liberty Song"

The Boston Massacre

On September 30, 1768, a fleet of British ships arrived in Boston Harbor carrying hundreds of soldiers. The soldiers marched off the ships wearing the bright red uniforms that led to their being called Redcoats or "lobster backs." They were also known as "regulars," the name for soldiers in a regular army.

The Bostonians hated their uninvited visitors. Few people would let the soldiers stay in their homes. At first, the troops camped on Boston Common, an open field in the center of the city. Later. they were housed in storage areas, lofts, and distilleries. Relations between the soldiers and the people of Boston were very bad. The soldiers, who were underpaid and probably frightened, were rude and sometimes even violent toward the Boston people. Fights were common and women were molested. Young boys teased the troops and sometimes received beatings in return. In 1769, customs men and soldiers savagely attacked James Otis, who had continued to protest against British tax laws.

In London, Lord North, who had became the British prime minister in 1770, said Boston was "in a state of disobedience to all law and government." North said he intended to bring the troublemakers to account.

On March 5, 1770, after a year and a half of the army's occupation of Boston, the tension between the Redcoats and the colonists came to a violent climax. Near the customs house, a boy insulted a British officer. A soldier then struck the boy with the butt of his rifle. The boy yelled out, and soon a crowd of several hundred people had gathered. A few more soldiers came to the scene, led by Captain Thomas Preston. Now the soldiers were confronted by an angry mob that hurled snowballs, ice, and garbage at them. One of the mob's leaders was a sailor and runaway slave named Crispus Attucks, who is thought to have been half black and half Indian. Some members of the mob stuck their faces in front of the soldiers' guns and dared them to fire. Then someone clubbed a soldier, knocking him to the

ground. He got up but was hit again, this time by a thrown club. He fired his gun, and within seconds other troops fired as well. The mob fled, but Attucks and four others lay on the ground, dead or dying. Several others were wounded.

The Boston Sons of Liberty outnumbered the British troops, and the city was threatened by even worse violence. The governor managed to quiet things by arresting the soldiers and announcing they would be put on trial for murder. At first, Preston and the other men could not find any lawyers to help with their defense. Eventually, however, John Adams and Josiah Quincy took up the case. Both lawyers were active in the protests, but they were convinced that every accused person had the right to legal defense.

Adams suffered jeers and rocks thrown through his window, but he and Quincy went ahead with defending the soldiers in the murder trial. They persuaded the jury that the soldiers had·acted in self-defense. Six were acquitted, and two were branded on their thumbs and then released.

The Sons of Liberty made sure that everyone heard about what they called "The Boston Massacre." Paul Revere, a Boston silversmith and engraver, made this engraving of the incident. It was printed in pamphlets and newspapers. Showing British soldiers firing on a peaceful group of people, the engraving gives a false picture of what actually happened.

John Adams (1735–1826)

John Adams was born in Braintree (now Quincy), Massachusetts. He was a great, great grandson of the Pilgrims John and Priscilla Alden, and a second cousin of Samuel Adams. Adams's father, a farmer and leather craftsman, taught him to read. Later, Adams went to Harvard College, where he developed a great love of books. He became a lawyer in 1758. Adams was stubborn and courageous, as his defense of the British soldiers involved in the Boston Massacre showed.

In 1764, Adams married Abigail Smith. Abigail was his equal in every respect, and their many letters testify to their close and loving relationship. One of their children was John Quincy Adams, who became president in 1825.

Adams served in the Massachusetts legislature from 1770 to 1774, and in the Continental Congresses from 1774 to 1777. In 1778, Congress sent him to represent the United States in several European countries. Adams was one of the people that negotiated the 1783 Treaty of Paris that ended the American Revolution.

John Adams became the nation's first vice president in 1789 and its second president in 1797. He died at home on the 50th anniversary of the Declaration of Independence. His old friend Thomas Jefferson died on the same day.

The End of the Townshend Acts

By chance, on the very day the Boston Massacre took place, Lord North asked British Parliament to repeal, or cancel, the Townshend Acts. British merchants were losing business because of the American boycott. Parliament kept in force only a small tax on tea. It was a matter of principle to show that it could tax the colonies in any way it chose. In America, the tea tax was generally ignored. It did not seem important because, since the boycott, many Americans bought Dutch tea. This was smuggled in and cost less than tea from Britain.

The repeal of the Townshend Acts came as a great relief. The boycotts against British goods were ended, and the next three years were somewhat calmer. However, people who had protested their rights against the British government remained cautious. They called themselves "Patriots." In many places, they formed "committees of correspondence" to keep in touch with other Patriots throughout the colonies.

Taxing Americans

Nowadays, most Americans accept that they have to pay taxes in one form or another. The money raised from taxes is what the national government and state and local governments use to pay for schools, roads, the United States armed forces, and many public services.

A major source of income for state governments is property tax. Everyone who owns land or buildings pays a yearly tax. The amount depends on the value of the property.

The stamp tax was a kind of sales tax, and we still pay sales tax today. Nearly all states add a tax to the price of cigarettes, alcohol, and gasoline. Some states add a sales tax to many other goods, and so we pay our state taxes when we buy those goods. In other states, people pay income tax (a tax on their earnings) instead of or in addition to sales tax.

The first time Americans paid income tax to the national government was in 1861, when it was introduced to help pay for the Civil War. But it was not until 1913 that the law allowed for income tax to be collected on a regular basis. Today, income tax is the national government's main source of funds.

From Tea Party to War

In May 1773, Parliament passed a new law called the Tea Act. This law led to renewed trouble between Britain and the American colonies, and then to open conflict.

The law was intended to help the British East India Company, which controlled all of Britain's trade with Asia. The company had nearly no money. It had large quantities of unsold tea sitting in its warehouses in Britain. To help get rid of it, the act allowed the East India Company to sell the tea directly to Americans at a low price, even with the tea tax included.

The Boston Tea Party

All over the colonies, people were furious. For one thing American tea importers would lose their business if the tea was sold directly to Americans instead of through them. Even worse was the idea that Americans were forced to buy the British tea. This meant they were paying the tea tax that they opposed.

At ports where British tea arrived by ship, people did everything they could to stop the tea from being landed or sold. In Philadelphia, no pilot would help the captain of the ship steer through the harbor and get the tea to shore. In Charleston, the tea was stored in moldy depots where it would rot.

The reaction was strongest in Boston, where three British ships docked with 45 tons (41 metric tons) of tea. Samuel Adams and other Sons of Liberty leaders addressed thousands of people in the streets. At town meetings, people promised

not to pay the tax. After a meeting on the night of December 16, 1773, the Sons of Liberty, badly disguised as Indians, boarded the tea ships. In three hours, they had opened the chests of tea and dumped all 45 tons into the water. During the event, which became known as the Boston Tea Party, there was no violence and no tea was taken by the men.

The Boston Tea Party began the chain of events that led directly to the American Revolution. The British government reacted harshly, and this in turn roused the colonists to further actions.

The Intolerable Acts

The Bostonians' bold act was cheered throughout the colonies. But the British government decided to make an example of Massachusetts and punish its "outrageous" behavior. In the spring of 1774, Parliament passed a group

21

of laws known as the Coercive Acts. Patriots thought them so harsh that they called them instead the "Intolerable Acts."

First, the port of Boston would be closed until all the destroyed tea was paid for. This was very serious because much of Boston's food arrived in the city by ship. Second, Massachusetts lost its self-government. Important officials and judges would be chosen by the British king or his governor in the colony, and they would be paid out of customs duties. Town meetings could only be held with the governor's permission. Next, no British officer or soldier accused of a crime in Massachusetts would be tried in the colony. Finally, more troops would be sent to the colony and had to be housed in people's homes. On May 13, four new regiments of British troops arrived in Boston, and more came soon after. General Thomas Gage, the British commander in America, was appointed governor of Massachusetts.

At the same time, Parliament passed the Quebec Act. This extended the boundaries of the Canadian province of Quebec southward to the Ohio River and westward to the Mississippi River. The law abolished claims that had previously been made by several American colonies to the territory west of the Ohio.

The British thought these firm measures would stop the protests, but they roused more protest than ever before. The Quebec Act and the Coercive Acts convinced the Patriots that the British were determined to take away their liberties. In Annapolis, Maryland, another "tea party" was held when residents dumped British tea overboard.

All the colonies felt threatened by Massachusetts' loss of self-government. They gave their support by sending food and other supplies overland to Boston. Sheep were sent from Connecticut, rye and bread from Maryland, and rice and flour from South Carolina and Virginia.

In Virginia, Patriots formed a new plan to boycott British goods again. The Virginia Committee of Correspondence invited the other colonies to send delegates to a meeting. They called the meeting a "Continental Congress."

"The cause of Boston, the despotick measures in respect to it, I mean, now is and ever will be considered as the cause of America."

George Washington, 1774

The First Continental Congress

On September 5, 1774, delegates from 12 of the 13 colonies arrived at the meeting in Philadelphia (which at the time was the largest city in America). Only Georgia, where a royal governor still controlled the colonial assembly, was not represented.

The 56 delegates were all white people, which was not surprising since blacks and Indians were not allowed to participate freely in colonial society. And they were all men. Women at that time took no role in public affairs.

The delegates came with different ideas. Some were fiery supporters of American rights; others were afraid of annoying Britain. But they all hoped to find an answer to the problems between the colonies and the mother country. Among them were some of the most outstanding colonists. Many would become very important in American history. The cousins Samuel and John Adams were in the delegation from Massachusetts. From New York came John Jay, who was more cautious in his views than either Adams. Virginia sent Richard Henry Lee and Patrick Henry, both firm believers in the colonies' right to govern themselves. Also representing Virginia was George Washington. Washington was quiet but highly respected for his judgment and military experience.

Meeting in Carpenter's Hall, the Congress opened on September 6. For more than seven weeks, the Congress discussed what to do.

Each colony had one vote on decisions. Joseph Galloway of Pennsylvania suggested a "Plan of Union" with Britain that would still leave Parliament with power over America. The delegates voted against this, although the vote was close. Instead they took several steps to assert American rights.

The Congress voted for a list of "resolves" from Massachusetts that suggested forming local militias. These would be groups of citizens trained for military service and ready to fight on short notice. Another step was to denounce the Coercive Acts and 13 other British laws. The Congress also passed a "Continental Association." This was an

"The distinctions between Virginians, Pennsylvanians, New Yorkers, and New Englanders, are no more. I am not a Virginian, but an American."

Patrick Henry, Continental Congress, 1774

Delegates from the British North American colonies pray at the opening of the Continental Congress in September 1774. For nearly two months, the delegates met in Carpenter's Hall, Philadelphia. They discussed ways to defend their rights, including forming local militia and banning British goods.

"Is life so dear, or peace so sweet, as to be purchased at the price of chains and slavery? Forbid it Almighty God! I know not what course others may take, but as for me, give me liberty, or give me death!"

Patrick Henry, at a Patriot meeting in Virginia, March 1775

agreement not to import British goods and not to export American goods to Britain. Committees would be created in local communities to make sure that the agreement was kept. Finally the Congress approved a "Declaration of Rights and Grievances" and a petition to the king.

The Continental Congress adjourned on October 25. It agreed to meet again in May 1775 if the problems had not been resolved.

Fighting Begins

By the fall of 1774, Patriots were taking up arms. Following Massachusetts' example, Rhode Island, Connecticut, Pennsylvania, Maryland, and Virginia organized companies of militia. The Patriots began to make stockpiles of weapons and ammunition. In Massachusetts, the militia formed companies of 50 men, called Minutemen. These men would be ready to report for action, if not in minutes, then at least in a few hours.

British leaders were also prepared for action. George III was ready to use force to

A gathering of militiamen at the beginning of the Revolutionary War shows a variety of uniforms and other clothing. Militia units from all over the colonies were soon to become part of the Continental Army, an army organized by Congress to fight the British.

Militia and Minutemen

Militia and Minutemen were nothing new to the American colonies. As far back as 1645, Massachusetts had soldiers "who shall be ready at half an hour's warning." They were used to defend the colony against Native American raids. Other colonies formed similar groups. After the defeat of the French in 1763, the militia organizations were not needed until the trouble with Britain began in the 1770s.

The Minutemen were the part of the militia that was always ready for battle. Each town was told to have one-third of its men between the ages of 16 and 30 "ready to act at a minute's warning." Each town had its own requirements. Lincoln, Massachusetts, for example, required its Minutemen to drill eight hours a week. Each Minuteman was supposed to be equipped with a musket, a bayonet, a cartridge box, and 36 rounds of ammunition. But only half the Patriot soldiers at the battles of Lexington and Concord in 1775 had bayonets. Many carried Indian-style hatchets instead.

Most of the militiamen were farmers, but there were also craftsmen and town workers. They elected their own officers, who were often professional men such as lawyers and doctors.

put down Patriot protests. Lord North directed General Gage to seize the "ringleaders of the riots at Boston." The British wanted most of all to capture Samuel Adams and John Hancock, who had a strong influence on people's opinions. It was said of them that "Sam Adams writes the letters and John Hancock pays the postage." The British also wanted to seize a supply of weapons that the Patriots had stored in Concord, a town 21 miles (34 km) inland and across the Charles River from Boston. (See map on page 28.)

Before dawn on April 19, 1775, a force of 800 British Redcoats under Major John Pitcairn set out quietly from Boston. Their orders were to go "with the utmost expediency and secrecy to Concord, where you will seize and destroy all the artillery and ammunition you can find." However, the movement of the troops was known to Patriot leaders even before they left Boston. The Patriots had many spies moving among the British. Servants, doctors, and perhaps even General Gage's American wife, all tried to find out any useful information they could.

Lexington and Concord

Adams and Hancock were in Lexington, directly on the route to Concord. The silversmith Paul Revere rushed on horseback to warn them. "The regulars are out!" Revere cried as he galloped through the night. Adams and Hancock left Lexington before dawn. A few hours later, nearly 80 Minutemen led by Captain John Parker stood waiting on the town green for the British troops. Among them were a 63-year-old, eight fathers with their sons, a slave named Prince Estabrook, and 12 teenagers.

The British were cold, tired, and hungry when they reached Lexington. Their leader Major Pitcairn yelled out to the Americans, "Lay down your arms, you damned rebels and disperse!" Greatly outnumbered, the Minuteman began to withdraw when somebody fired a shot. The Redcoats then fired into the ranks of the Americans, killing eight. The Minutemen returned fire but soon retreated.

"We were fired on from all sides, but mostly from the rear, where people hid themselves in houses till we had passed. . . . Their numbers [were] increasing from all parts, while ours [were] reducing by deaths, wounds, and fatigue . . ."

A British lieutenant at Concord, April 1775

The British continued on to Concord. Throughout the area, however, church bells had been alerting the Patriot militia. The Americans had time to bury their supplies in Concord, and militia began converging on the town. The British were unable to find the weapons and ammunition they were looking for in Concord, even after a house-to-house search. At the North Bridge over the Concord River, they battled a company of militia, killing two and suffering three deaths themselves. Then they left Concord at midday to return to Boston.

The journey was a road of horror for the British. Word of the events at Lexington and North Bridge had spread. From behind trees, bushes, rocks, walls, and barns, Americans poured fire on the Redcoats. A British corporal recalled, "A grait many Lay dead and the Road was bloddy." After a couple of hours, reinforcements arrived to help the British. Then the British burned and looted buildings along their path. In one town, Patriots and Redcoats fought hand-to-hand, and there were many deaths on both sides. In that one day, an estimated 3,700 Patriot militia had fought 1,800 British. By the time they reached Boston, the Redcoats had lost 272 dead and wounded. How many Patriots were wounded is not exactly known, but there were about 50 men killed.

In 1847, the great American philosopher and poet Ralph Waldo Emerson published a poem about the battle at North Bridge (above). The poem's most famous lines are these:
"By the rude bridge that arched the flood,
Their flag to freedom's breeze unfurled,
Here once the embattled farmers stood
And fired the shot heard 'round the world."

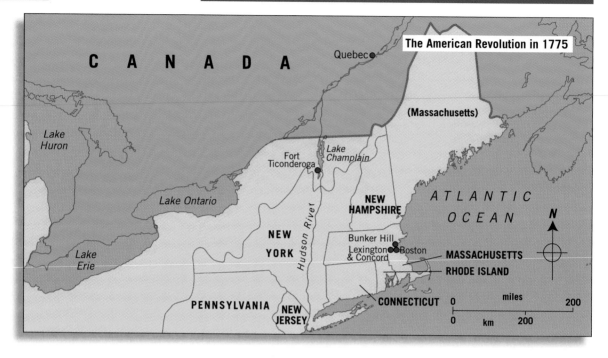

The American Revolution in 1775

This map shows where the first major battles of the American Revolution were fought during 1775.

The militiamen of Massachusetts now began to position themselves in units around Boston. Additional units came from other New England colonies, and soon there were 10,000 men. On the British side, Governor-General Gage had his men build fortifications in the city. The war of the American Revolution had begun.

On May 10, 1775, Patriot militia captured the British base of Fort Ticonderoga, on Lake Champlain in New York. The militia consisted of two groups. One was from western Massachusetts, led by Benedict Arnold. The other group was from what is now Vermont. They were called the Green Mountain Boys and were led by Ethan Allen. Fort Ticonderoga was an important strategic point between the Hudson River and Canada. Moreover, it had a large supply of artillery and ammunition, which Arnold wanted to take to the Patriots around Boston. About 500 Americans overwhelmed the small British garrison at the fort, who were totally surprised by the attack. According to one account, Allen called on the commanding officer to surrender "in the name of the great Jehovah and the Continental Congress."

The Second Continental Congress

On the very day that Ethan Allen invoked its name, the Continental Congress met again in Philadelphia. It was three weeks after the fateful events at Lexington and Concord.

This time, all 13 colonies were represented, although the delegates from Georgia, the southernmost colony, arrived late. Many of the delegates to the First Congress—including John and Samuel Adams, Patrick Henry, Richard Henry Lee, and George Washington, who appeared in military uniform—were back. There were also some important newcomers at the second Congress.

Benjamin Franklin had recently returned from England, where he had been a representative for several colonies. He was probably the most famous American in the world at that time. Another well-known new delegate was the wealthy John Hancock, whom the British had tried to arrest just a few weeks earlier. To snub the British, the delegates chose Hancock as President of the Congress. Also new was a 32-year-old from Virginia, Thomas Jefferson.

The delegates faced very serious issues. Americans and British had now been killed in fighting. Both sides were preparing for a major battle for Boston. Patriots in Massachusetts had appealed to the Congress for help. After spending nearly a month debating whether to send another petition to the king, Congress took a big step on June 14. It decided to reorganize the militia units around Boston into a single American force. The new force was called the "Continental Army." Companies of riflemen and infantry from Pennsylvania, Maryland, and Virginia were to go to Boston to join the force.

The Continental Army needed a commander in chief, and John Adams nominated George Washington. The next day, Washington was unanimously approved, although he said "I do not think myself equal to the command." He turned down a regular salary, and asked only to be paid for his expenses. Congress also chose other officers for the army.

George Washington (1732–99)

George Washington was born in Virginia. He was one of five children and also had two half-brothers and a half-sister from his father's first marriage. After his father died when George was 11, he was brought up at Mount Vernon, the home of his half-brother Lawrence. Washington was well read and good at mathematics, and he trained to become a land surveyor.

Washington was very dignified and had excellent judgment. Above all, he was a person of unquestioned honesty. He was over six feet tall and very muscular. His face was scarred from the smallpox he caught on a trip to Barbados when a young man.

Washington married Martha Dandridge Custis, a wealthy widow with two children, in 1759. The marriage of Martha and George was a happy one, although they had no children of their own.

Washington probably had the most military experience of anyone in America. He had fought in the French and Indian War as a member of the Virginia militia. He then took command of the Continental Army at the beginning of the American Revolution in 1775.

Washington went home to Mount Vernon only twice in the following eight years. When the war ended in 1783, Washington wanted to spend the rest of his life at home. But he agreed to attend the 1787 Constitutional Convention in Philadelphia, and was chosen as the Convention's president. After the new Constitution was accepted, Washington was elected the first president of the United States in 1789. He retired in 1797 after serving two terms as president, and died two years later at Mount Vernon. In his will, Washington provided for the freeing of his slaves after the death of his wife. Martha Washington died in 1801.

In several ways, the Second Continental Congress began acting as the government of the colonies. It took steps to print money and create a post office. It also began to establish relations with American Indian tribes and with foreign governments.

Compromise Fails

But what were the colonies' relations with Britain to be? The delegates were divided. Some, like the Adamses and Patrick Henry, favored independence for America. But nobody spoke of this as yet. John Dickinson of Delaware thought they should be careful. He and others said the colonists should pay for the destroyed tea and allow Parliament to regulate American trade. Then they could petition the king to respect the colonies' rights. Others disagreed. They would accept the king as their sovereign, but not that a British Parliament should govern America.

After much discussion, Congress, as the Continental Congress was now called, approved two documents in July 1775. The documents somewhat contradicted each other. The first, written by Dickinson and Jefferson, was the "Declaration of the Causes and Necessity for Taking Up Arms." The second, by Dickinson alone, was a petition to the king, known as the Olive Branch Petition.

The compromise did not work. When the Olive Branch Petition reached Britain in August, King George III refused even to read it. The British government prepared instead to wage war against the Americans. The king proclaimed the colonies to be in "open rebellion."

The Second Continental Congress met in what is now Independence Hall, Philadelphia. At that time, it was known as the Pennsylvania State House. The building housed the Liberty Bell, which was rung when the Declaration of Independence was approved there in 1776. The bell became too cracked to use in 1846, and is now kept at the Liberty Bell Pavilion in Philadelphia.

Bunker Hill and Boston

While Congress debated, the situation around Boston grew more serious. The city was becoming an armed camp. Many of the inhabitants fled. The British controlled the sea approaches to Boston, while the Patriots held the land routes. On May 25, 1775, British troops arrived. They were accompanied by three experienced generals: William Howe, Henry Clinton, and John Burgoyne. On June 12, Governor-General Gage offered to pardon all Patriots who gave up their weapons, but the offer was ignored.

Whoever could occupy the hills to the north and southeast of Boston could control the city. On the night of June 16, 1,200 Patriot militia seized what is mistakenly called Bunker Hill. It was actually Breed's Hill, on the Charlestown Neck, a peninsula north of Boston. (See map on page 28.) The British thought the Americans would be no match for their experienced regulars, and decided to drive them off the hill. They began an artillery barrage against the hill the next

When the American Revolution began, the British were short of troops. They hired soldiers from Germany to go and fight in America. Some of the soldiers were from the part of Germany called Hesse-Cassel, and became known as "Hessians." They wore blue jackets (left), while the British wore the red coats that gave them their name.

morning. Charlestown, a neighboring town, was destroyed. In the middle of the afternoon, General Howe sent 2,000 men on 40 barges across the Charles River to storm the hill. Patriot officers instructed their men not to fire at the Redcoats until they could "see the whites of their eyes. . . . Pick off the commanders—aim at the handsome coats."

On that fiercely hot day, each British soldier laboring up the hill was carrying more than 100 pounds (37 kg) of supplies on his back. Twice the British columns started up the hill, and twice deadly fire from the Patriots drove them back. On the third attempt, the Patriots ran out of ammunition and were forced to give up the position. The British took Bunker Hill, but they lost more than 1,000 men, including 92 officers. American losses were heavy too: 150 killed and 300 wounded. However, the Americans had shown the British that they had a real fight on their hands.

The Americans had begun to fortify their position on Breed's Hill (which actually was nearer to Boston than Bunker Hill) when the British began their attack. Charlestown, opposite Boston and right next to the fighting, caught fire during the battle.

Washington arrived in Massachusetts in early July to take command of the Continental Army. He had a long and difficult task ahead to turn the Patriot soldiers into a fighting force. The American troops were growing in numbers every day and were full of enthusiasm, but they lacked discipline, organization, and leadership. They badly needed supplies of all kinds: clothing, medicine, blankets, tents, and cooking utensils. As Bunker Hill had shown, they were also short of ammunition. Making his headquarters in Cambridge, across the Charles River from Boston, Washington began the hard work of shaping the Patriot fighters into an army.

By March 1776, the new Continental Army was ready for action. The weapons captured at Fort Ticonderoga finally arrived. But before the Americans could attack the British positions in Boston, on March 17 the Redcoats left the city. The British sailed north to their base at Halifax, Nova Scotia. That same day, the Continental Army entered Boston.

The British Empire

The American colonies were only one part of the British Empire. The size and power of the empire grew bigger and smaller over several centuries. At its largest, just before the start of World War I in 1914, the British Empire's population was one quarter of the entire world's.

In the 1600s and 1700s, Britain competed with other European nations for control of huge areas of the world. After the American Revolution, the British kept control of their colonies in Canada and expanded into other parts of the world. They started settlements in Australia and New Zealand and acquired territories in the Far East. By the end of the 19th century, Britain also controlled most of the Indian subcontinent and much of eastern and southern Africa.

But even as the empire grew, some parts of it were moving toward self-government. Canada, Australia, New Zealand, and South Africa became independent in 1931. At the same time they and Britain became the founding members of the Commonwealth of Nations. Other colonies joined the Commonwealth as they, too, gained their independence.

3

America Declares Its Independence

By the spring of 1776, fighting between British and Americans had been going on for a year. Besides the action around Boston and the capture of Fort Ticonderoga in 1775, there were battles at several other places in North America.

Warfare in Canada and the South

Congress was worried that there might be a British invasion from Canada. In the summer of 1775, the Americans decided to mount an attack on Canada from Fort Ticonderoga. A force of about 1,000 men under Richard Montgomery captured Montreal, Canada, in November. Then in early December, Montgomery's army joined with a smaller force led by Benedict Arnold. Arnold's men had endured terrible hardships on their journey from Massachusetts. Hunger drove them to eat a dog, leather goods, soap, and even hair cream.

The combined American force attacked Quebec on December 31, but met with disaster. Montgomery was killed, Arnold was wounded, and hundreds of soldiers were taken prisoner. Arnold managed to hold his men together outside of Quebec through the bitter Canadian winter. Although reinforcements arrived in the spring, the British again defeated the Americans. The wounded Patriots made it back to Fort Ticonderoga in July 1776.

There were also battles in the Southern Colonies. The royal governor of Virginia, Lord Dunmore, made his headquarters in Norfolk and tried to organize an army of Virginians loyal to Britain. He promised freedom to Virginia's slaves if they would fight for Britain. Several hundred black men became the "Loyal Ethiopian Regiment."

The British appeal to the slaves encouraged white Virginians to side with the Patriots. The Americans defeated the British force, and Dunmore fled to a British warship off Norfolk. On New Year's Day 1776, Dunmore ordered the navy to bombard Norfolk. Much of the town was destroyed.

Later in January, the British general Sir Henry Clinton sailed for North Carolina from Halifax with 2,000 troops. There were bitter conflicts among the Carolina colonists. Immigrants to North Carolina from the Scottish Highlands were loyal to the king and had formed an army. In a battle on February 27, 1776, at Moore's Bridge near Wilmington, they were defeated by a Patriot army of Scotch-Irish frontiersmen.

The battle occurred just days before Clinton's force arrived at the North Carolina coast. Clinton's troops joined another British force led by Lord Charles Cornwallis, and decided to attack Charleston, South Carolina. Washington sent General Charles Lee down to lead the Patriot defense. The British attacked on June 28, but they were driven off. The British had also planned Indian attacks on frontier settlements in the Carolinas, Georgia, and Virginia. These attacks failed, and the Patriots retaliated by destroying Native American villages.

When the British force attacked Charleston in June 1776, the Patriots successfully defended the city. The sturdy logs of Fort Moultrie protected the Americans from British artillery fire.

Common Sense

While all these events were taking place, Congress remained in session in Philadelphia. Managing the growing war took up much of its attention. But from several colonies came urgent questions of a different kind.

The royal governors had been dissolving assemblies as the British Parliament ended colonial self-government. So the colonies had been forming their own governing bodies. Now they were asking Congress for advice. What was the role of these new assemblies, and what was their relationship to Britain?

The group in Congress that believed in independence from Britain were thought of as "radicals," meaning people who wanted to make extreme changes. They believed each colony should form a new government. Then the colonies should get together as a confederation and declare their independence. Most of the delegates were still "moderates," which meant they did not want such huge changes. They believed America should assert its rights, but they hoped to remain part of the British Empire.

However, the moderates began to change their minds as the battles raged and more American blood was shed. It was clear the British government was not going to back down, and the radical view grew stronger in Congress.

Into this uncertainty came a powerful appeal, like a bolt of lightning. In January 1776, a recent immigrant from Britain named Thomas Paine published a pamphlet in Philadelphia. The pamphlet was called *Common Sense.*

Paine argued that both the king and Parliament had been conspiring to destroy American rights. Stop following the "royal brute," Paine said. "The cause of America is . . . the cause of all mankind."

"Every thing that is right or natural pleads for separation. The blood of the slain, the weeping voice of nature cries, "TIS TIME TO PART."

Thomas Paine, 1776, in Common Sense

In Common Sense, *Thomas Paine offered "simple facts, plain argument, and common sense." He said in strong, clear language that America should be independent of Britain.*

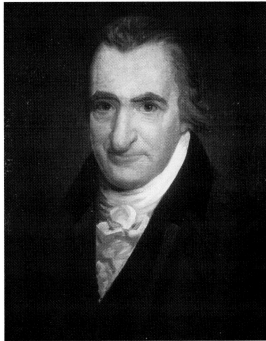

Thomas Paine (1737–1809)

Thomas Paine was born in Thetford, England. He received little education and at the age of 16 ran away to become a sailor. After that he flitted from one job to another: corsetmaker (like his father), teacher, shopkeeper, tax collector. Paine was married twice but had no children.

In London Paine met Benjamin Franklin who advised him to go to America. He did this in 1774, where he had a great success with his pamphlet *Common Sense*. Paine then wrote *The Crisis*, which were essays to lift the spirits of the Patriots after several defeats. In addition to his successful writings, Paine designed a new kind of iron bridge. But he was almost always a failure in practical life, and never earned a cent from his writings.

After the American Revolution, Paine went back to England. He continued to write about public affairs in a way that shocked some people. He was exiled to France, where he became involved in the French Revolution.

Paine returned to the United States in 1801. By this time his political and religious views had made him quite unpopular. In the last years before his death in New York, he became a penniless alcoholic.

"That these United Colonies are, and of right ought to be, free and independent States . . . and that all political connection between them and the State of Great Britain is, and ought to be, totally dissolved."

Richard Henry Lee, June 7, 1776

Common Sense had tremendous impact. Within three months of its publication, more than 100,000 copies were sold. That would be like selling several million copies today.

Independence

As winter turned to spring in 1776, the idea of independence gained support throughout the colonies. In March, the assemblies of South Carolina and Georgia told their delegates to support independence. On April 12, the North Carolina assembly followed suit.

Around this time, the news arrived that Britain was hiring thousands of Hessians to fight in America. Some colonists found this very offensive. On May 10, Congress formally recommended to the colonies that they form new

governments. Rhode Island declared its own independence that month. On May 15, the Virginia assembly told its delegates in Congress to propose independence.

On June 7, Virginia's Richard Henry Lee rose in Congress and suggested a history-making resolution. He proposed that the colonies should become independent states and break off all connection to Britain. He also said that the colonies should make alliances with foreign countries. Lastly, he said that the colonies should make a plan for uniting themselves.

Some colonies, especially the "middle" ones, were not yet ready for such a step. Others were worried about the order of events in the resolution. Edward Rutledge of South Carolina, for example, was worried that the colonies would appear ridiculous to foreign governments if they tried to make alliances "before we had united with each other."

No decision on the independence resolution was made right away. June 1776 must have been a difficult month for the delegates in Philadelphia. While they considered their important vote, one piece of bad news after another arrived. They learned that Parliament had passed a law making trade with America illegal. This meant the Royal Navy would seize any ship carrying goods to or from the colonies. Then Congress received the details of the defeat in Canada. (News traveled very slowly in those days.) They knew an attack on Charleston, South Carolina, could happen any minute. And, on June 29, a British fleet was sighted off New York City.

In 1776, Virginia recommended to Congress that the colonies declare their independence from Britain. In June of that year, at a constitutional convention (above), Virginia became the first of the colonies to write a state constitution for itself.

By June 28, all the colonies except New York had told their delegates to vote for independence. But when debate began again in Congress on July 1, a hot day with thunderstorms, some of those delegates still hesitated. Unfortunately, no records were kept of this historic occasion. We do know that John Adams spoke eloquently for independence, and John Dickinson against.

Pennsylvania and South Carolina were still opposed, and Delaware was split. New Yorkers wanted to vote for independence but their instructions didn't allow them to. The next day, Pennsylvania and South Carolina decided to support independence. A third delegate from Delaware arrived, having ridden 80 miles (128 km) overnight through the rain. His vote put Delaware on the side of independence, too.

On July 2, 1776, Congress was at last able to approve Richard Henry Lee's resolution. Except for New York, the vote was unanimous. (New York did not vote that day, but on July 15, it also approved.)

The Declaration of Independence

A committee had already been appointed to write a declaration of independence. On the committee were Thomas Jefferson, Benjamin Franklin, John Adams, Roger Sherman of Connecticut, and Robert Livingston of New York. Jefferson and Adams were given the task of actually writing the declaration. Between themselves, they decided Jefferson should do it.

Jefferson spent about two weeks in June writing and rewriting his draft. When it was finished, he showed it to Franklin and Adams, who made a few changes in wording. The draft was read to Congress on June 28. Congress made some changes and shortened the draft, but kept most of Jefferson's work. Congress approved the Declaration on July 4. So the day we celebrate as America's "birthday" is actually the day the Declaration of Independence was approved, not independence itself.

Thomas Jefferson (1743–1826)

Thomas Jefferson was born and raised near Charlottesville, Virginia, in sight of the Blue Ridge Mountains. He had one brother and six sisters. When Jefferson was 14, his father died.

Jefferson attended William and Mary College in Williamsburg, Virginia. He became a lawyer and in 1769 was chosen as a member of the Virginia House of Burgesses. In 1772, he married Martha Wayles Skelton, a wealthy widow. Martha died 10 years later. Only two of their numerous children survived beyond childhood.

When Jefferson first came to the Continental Congress in 1775, he was already known as a skilled writer. Soon after writing the Declaration of Independence, Jefferson returned to Virginia to work in the legislature reforming the state's laws. After much struggle, Virginia passed his bill for religious freedom. But his proposals for a system of public education and for the gradual freeing of Virginia's slaves were defeated. Later in life, Jefferson seemed to lose interest in the antislavery cause, and he always doubted that blacks were the mental equal of whites. He served as governor of Virginia from 1779 to 1781.

The tragedy of his wife's death caused Jefferson to retire from public life in the early 1780s. But he returned to Congress in 1783 and became the U.S. minister to France in 1785. President Washington appointed him secretary of state in 1789. In 1797, Jefferson became vice president, and in 1801 he was elected president.

Jefferson was a very talented man, with many interests. Toward the end of his long life, he founded the University of Virginia. He died on July 4, 1826, the same day as John Adams. It was the 50th anniversary of the Declaration of Independence.

Jefferson reads a draft of the Declaration of Independence to Benjamin Franklin.

Only the Congress president, John Hancock, and the secretary, Charles Thomson, signed the original Declaration of Independence on July 4, 1776. A parchment copy was later made that was signed by the delegates of the newly independent states.

The Declaration was printed, and over the next few weeks all the delegates signed it. The first to sign was John Hancock, the President of the Congress, whose large signature may still be clearly seen today.

Congress sent copies of the Declaration to all the colonies and to the officers of the Continental Army. Celebrations were held throughout the new United Colonies of America. (Congress officially changed the name from "United Colonies" to "United States" on September 9.) Washington ordered the Declaration read to his troops on July 9. In New York City, people tore down a statue of George III, and the metal was later made into ammunition.

The Meaning of the Declaration

The Declaration of Independence has two main parts, and a brief introduction and conclusion. The introduction simply states that Americans wish to explain to the world why they were doing what they were doing. The first main part contains the words that many Americans know by heart. These are words that have inspired people all over the world ever since they were written.

The second, longest section of the Declaration is a list of the wrongs that the Patriots believed Britain had committed against America. The British, it says, intended to impose "an absolute Tyranny over these States." This was done in many ways, from imposing taxes to cutting off trade and waging war. Congress deleted some of Jefferson's original complaints, including one that blamed the British king for bringing slavery to America.

The final draft of the Declaration of Independence is presented to John Hancock by Thomas Jefferson at Independence Hall. This painting is by John Trumbull, a leading American artist of the time.

43

"We hold these truths to be self-evident, that all men are created equal, that they are endowed by their Creator with certain unalienable Rights, that among these are Life, Liberty, and the pursuit of Happiness. That to secure these rights, Governments are instituted among Men, deriving their just powers from the consent of the governed. That whenever any Form of Government becomes destructive of these ends, it is the Right of the People to alter or to abolish it and to institute new Government, laying its foundations on such principles and organizing its powers in such form, as to them shall seem most likely to effect their Safety and Happiness."

Declaration of Independence, 1776

The Declaration concludes by stating the colonies are "free and independent states." In support of that, the delegates "pledge to each other our Lives, our fortunes, and our sacred Honor."

It is the first main section, however, that has made the Declaration immortal. Here, to justify what they were doing, the delegates presented their ideas of human rights, government, and revolution. Since they were breaking ties with Britain, they could not claim their rights as British citizens any longer. Instead, as Thomas Paine did in *Common Sense*, they relied on the ideas of the Enlightenment movement. The Declaration of Independence says that mankind's rights are God-given. If these natural rights are violated, then revolution may be justified. This important idea has had a great influence on the history of the United States and the rest of the world.

Liberty and Equality?

The words "all men are created equal" and are entitled to the rights of "Life, Liberty, and the pursuit of Happiness" are often quoted today. They still represent what most Americans believe about society.

What do these words mean? What exactly did Jefferson mean by them? Did he intend them to apply to all people everywhere? To blacks, Native Americans, and women, or only to white men? We do not know the answers for sure. Jefferson and his colleagues may have meant "all people are equal in God's eyes." Or simply that Americans were the equal of the British. They may not even have thought of equality as we think of it now. They were declaring principles to encourage the American people in their struggle for independence. And ever since July 1776, many Americans have tried to make these principles a reality.

4

Defeats and Victories

In the early days of the American Revolution, people on both the American and British sides expected the conflict to be a short one. Many Patriots thought that after they whipped the British once or twice, King George and his government would agree to leave them alone. George Washington, however, thought a waiting strategy was best. If he could keep his own army going, Washington thought the British would eventually tire of the struggle. Time, Washington felt, was on the Americans' side.

On the other side, the British thought that one decisive victory would bring the Americans to their senses and make them forget their foolish notions of independence. The battle at Bunker Hill, however, had caused some British leaders to change their minds.

The British Advantages

At first it looked as if the British had all the advantages. They had the strongest navy in the world and a well-trained army. Britain's population of 9 million people was more than three times that of America, and it was backed by the wealth of a huge empire.

The Americans had almost no navy. Their army had little experience and they were low on weapons and ammunition. Congress was always short of money, and so it had trouble buying supplies and paying soldiers. Many men joined the Continental Army only for short periods and then returned home. The army's strength went up and down, and Washington often appealed to the states for more troops. But

"On our side, the war should be defensive. . . . We should on all occasions avoid a general action, and never be drawn into a necessity to put anything at risk. . . . When the fate of America may be at stake on the issue, we should protract the war, if possible."

Washington to Congress, September 1776

45

THE PART OF THE TOWN OF BOSTON IN NEW ENGLAND AND BRITISH SHIPS OF WAR LANDING THEIR TROOPS

The British navy was a powerful presence from the beginning of the conflict, when a large fleet arrived in Boston Harbor carrying British soldiers. In addition to using their ships to attack the Patriots, the British could blockade American ports and carry large numbers of soldiers to where they were needed.

the state militia were not always reliable and also served only for short periods of time.

Not all Americans supported the war for independence. Many Native Americans sided with the British, although Congress appealed to them not to take sides. The Indians believed that British rule posed less of a threat to their lands than American rule. Some tribes remained neutral, while only a few tribes supported the Patriots.

White Americans were also divided in their attitude to the Revolution. Some people, called "Loyalists" or "Tories," sided with Britain. There were as many as 500,000 Loyalists, nearly a fifth of the total population. Perhaps as many as 100,000 left America during the war and went to live in Canada, Britain, or the West Indies. Some never returned.

Loyalists lived mostly in the middle states and the Carolinas. They were fewest in Virginia and New England. They included farmers in the Hudson valley, many Dutch people in New York and New Jersey, Germans and Quakers (who opposed all fighting) in Pennsylvania, and Scottish people in the Carolinas. Some people were loyal to Britain because they were members of the Church of England, and others just because they disliked the change and turmoil the Revolution brought. Some Loyalists were dependent on the British for jobs or income. Others simply could not understand what all the fuss was about.

Friends and families were split. William Franklin, son of the Patriot leader Benjamin Franklin, was a Loyalist. He had been the royal governor of New Jersey and was arrested by the state assembly and forced to leave the state. John Hancock's brother-in-law was a Loyalist. Thousands of Loyalists fought on the British side, and battles between Loyalists and Patriots were especially bitter.

Other people, of course, took no side and just went about their business. Some changed their minds as the war progressed, or when one or another army happened to be in the vicinity. In Poughkeepsie, New York, it was said there were 101 "committed" Patriots, 61 "staunch" Loyalists, 29 "occasional" Patriots, and 40 "occasional" Loyalists.

> "Neighbor was against Neighbor, father against son and son against father. He that would not thrust his own blade through his brother's heart was called an infamous villain."
>
> *A Connecticut Loyalist*

Even in small towns, loyalties were divided. The man being carried is a Loyalist who has been denounced by Patriots and banished from his town.

The American Advantages

The Patriots did have some advantages in the war, even though these were not so obvious. Generally their morale was high because they believed they were fighting for their liberty. And they were to receive powerful support from other nations.

The Patriots were also fighting on their own land, a large country with a coastline 1,800 miles (2,896 km) long. The British would need very large forces to regain control in all that territory. They would have to bring most of those forces a very long way, 3,000 miles (4,827 km) across the Atlantic Ocean. In spite of its large population, Britain was short of men, too. Parliament tried to recruit 55,000 British troops to fight in America but in the end had to send 30,000 Hessians to make up the numbers.

A large number of British people and some respected leaders sympathized with the Patriot cause. Critics warned of the difficulty of defeating the Americans.

The Patriots also enjoyed the supreme good fortune of having George Washington as their leader. The British had no one to match him. Washington's skill and determination, and the respect people had for him, had a tremendous influence on the outcome of the struggle.

Battles in New York and New Jersey

When the British left Boston and sailed for Halifax, Nova Scotia, in March 1776, Washington was sure they would soon be back. He suspected that New York City would be their target.

Washington was correct. The British plan was to split the new nation in two by separating New England from the states south of it. To do this, they had to capture New York City. On July 2, British forces poured into New York Harbor. Hundreds of ships arrived, bringing thousands of troops commanded by General Howe. When Clinton's army joined them from Charleston, South Carolina, the British had close to 30,000 men. Their fleet could control all the waterways of the city. They made their headquarters on Staten Island. (See map on page 52.)

Nathan Hale (1755–76)

Nathan Hale was one of the heroes of the American Revolution. Hale was a schoolteacher from Connecticut. He enlisted in the militia when the Revolution began and became a captain.

The Connecticut militia took part in the fighting around New York City. Washington needed spies to go behind the British lines and find out what their plans were. Hale volunteered and disguised himself as a Dutch schoolmaster. He moved among the British camps in Brooklyn and followed them when they crossed into Manhattan in September 1776.

The British became more careful after the Americans started a fire in Manhattan to slow them down. They discovered Hale's true identity on September 20, and suspected he was involved in setting the fire. The British executed Hale by hanging him two days later. His famous last words were, "I only regret that I have but one life to lose for my country." His last letters were destroyed by a British officer who said, "The rebels should never know they had a man who could die with so much firmness."

The execution of Nathan Hale.

Washington takes a gamble in December 1776, at a low point of the American Revolution. Having retreated to Pennsylvania two weeks before, the Patriot army recrossed the Delaware River on a stormy night. The Americans then made surprise attacks on several Hessian camps in New Jersey.

Washington had moved the Continental Army from Boston to New York in April. He wrote his brother on May 31, "We expect a very bloody summer of it." With fewer than 20,000 troops and no navy, Washington tried to fortify positions in and around the city, hoping to stop the British from capturing it.

The struggle for New York began on August 22, 1776, with the Battle of Long Island. Fifteen thousand British troops stormed American positions. Over the next few days, the Patriots fell back again and again. Had Howe pushed harder, the British might have won the war right there. But he remembered the terrible losses at Bunker Hill and proceeded very cautiously.

Washington managed to withdraw his army across the East River to Manhattan on August 30. The British followed. More battles took place and the Continental Army barely managed to avoid destruction. With the British in pursuit, the Americans retreated across the Hudson River and through New Jersey in November. In early December, they crossed the Delaware River to Pennsylvania. Washington destroyed all the boats in the area not needed by his army.

This move finally stopped the British from following, but there had been a humiliating series of defeats. Deaths and desertions left the Continental Army with only a few thousand men. More were scheduled to leave when their enlistments were up at the end of December. Washington was deeply discouraged, but determined to keep the Patriot cause alive.

After making camp across the Delaware in December, Washington noticed that the British had scattered their forces in New Jersey. He saw a chance to surprise them. On Christmas night, he led a few thousand troops back across the icy Delaware. The next morning, he surprised the British at Trenton. The Americans captured about 900 Hessians and quickly returned across the river. "It was a glorious day," Washington said.

At the start of 1777, the Continental Army had shrunk to only about 1,600 men. Fortunately for the Americans, just then 3,600 militia arrived from Pennsylvania. And after Washington offered to pay their salaries out of his own pocket, 1,300 Continental soldiers agreed to stay on.

From British headquarters in New York, Howe ordered General Cornwallis to deal with Washington. Cornwallis was confident he could "bag the fox." He arrived in Princeton on January 1 with 8,000 troops. Leaving about 1,000 men there, he marched the rest on to Trenton, where Washington and his troops were. But Washington evaded the main force and attacked the troops left at Princeton instead. After a short but fierce fight, the British fled, leaving 300 men as prisoners.

For the rest of the winter, the Continental Army camped at Morristown, New Jersey. Washington succeeded in making the British army think he had many more troops than he did, and because of this the British kept their distance.

Paine's *The Crisis*

Thomas Paine, the author of *Common Sense*, had been with the Continental Army as it retreated across New Jersey. Hoping to raise the Patriots' sinking spirits, he started writing a series of essays called *The Crisis*. The first of these essays appeared in December 1776.

"These are the times that try men's souls. The summer soldier and the sunshine patriot will in this crisis shrink from the service of their country; but he that stands it now deserves the love and thanks of man and woman. Tyranny, like Hell, is not easily conquered; yet we have this consolation with us, that the harder the conflict, the more glorious the triumph. . . . Heaven knows how to put a proper price upon its goods; and it would be strange indeed if so celestial an article as freedom should not be highly rated."

Washington had Paine's stirring words read to his troops.

A Turning Point

Meanwhile, the British were working out a grand scheme. They expected it to end the war once and for all. General Burgoyne would lead a force of about 8,000, plus Native American allies, south from St. Johns, Canada. A second force under Lieutenant Colonel Barry St. Leger would move eastward from Oswego on Lake Ontario. St. Leger's army included many Iroquois led by the Mohawk chief Joseph Brant. A third force led by General Howe would move up the Hudson River from New York City.

As battles raged in New York and New Jersey, and after the failure of the British plan to divide the colonies, the tide seemed to be turning in favor of the Patriots.

All three armies would meet at Albany, New York. In this way, the new United States would be split in two.

Starting in mid-June 1777, Burgoyne did well at first. He captured Fort Ticonderoga on July 5. But then Burgoyne's progress became slow. The Redcoats got stuck in dense forest as the Patriot militia chopped down trees in their path. Burgoyne also lost one-tenth of his army when they were ambushed by the Green Mountain Boys from Vermont.

Meanwhile, St. Leger's force retreated to Canada after a battle at Fort Stanwix on the Mohawk River. Even worse, Howe decided to capture Philadelphia instead of moving north to link up with Burgoyne. He sailed from New York on July 31. Delayed by storms, he landed 50 miles (80 km) south of Philadelphia in mid-August.

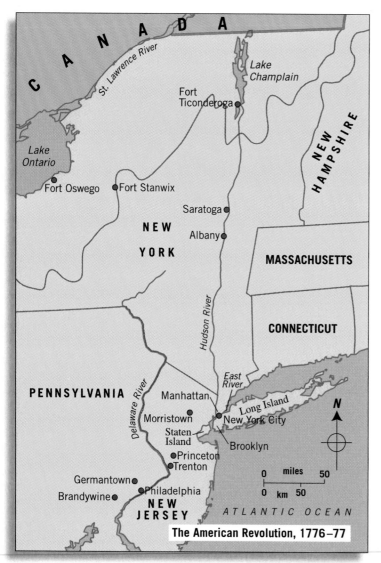

The American Revolution, 1776–77

From New Jersey, Washington had been watching Howe and preparing to stop him from linking up with Burgoyne. Now he raced south to defend Philadelphia. But he was unsuccessful. In a battle at Brandywine Creek on September 11, the Americans were forced to retreat. The British entered Philadelphia on September 26, 1777. Congress had already fled to York, Pennsylvania. Washington attacked the British camp at Germantown, outside Philadelphia on October 4. It was a very foggy day. The Americans were on the verge of a victory when, in the fog, two Patriot divisions began firing on each other. Once again, Washington had to withdraw.

Meanwhile, however, Burgoyne was in trouble in New York State. The great British plan to split America had fallen apart. The forces that were to join Burgoyne from the west and south had not arrived. His army was shrinking and he was running out of vital supplies. The Patriot army opposing him was growing every day as more militia and regulars arrived.

The Americans blocked the British army's route at a position just south of Saratoga, New York. Retreating to Saratoga, Burgoyne was now surrounded by a force three times larger than his own.

Seeing no way out, Burgoyne surrendered on October 17. He told the Patriot commander General Horatio Gates, "The

At Saratoga, British General Burgoyne was allowed to surrender with great dignity. He handed his sword to Patriot General Gates, who then immediately returned it. And although Burgoyne's men had to surrender their arms, they did so with full honors.

Marquis de Lafayette (1757–1834)

In 1777, foreign support for the American cause came in the form of a talented young Frenchman, the Marquis de Lafayette. He was born in France, the son of aristocrats. He entered the French Army in 1771, but resigned at the age of 19 to come to America.

Lafayette arrived in America on June 13, 1777, with recommendation letters from Benjamin Franklin and others. He offered to serve in the Continental Army without pay. Congress made him a major general, and he donated a large sum of money to buy supplies for the army.

Lafayette impressed almost everyone he met. He quickly became a great favorite of Washington. When he was wounded at the Battle of Brandywine in 1777, Washington told the army doctor, "Treat him as if he were my son, for I love him as if he were." Lafayette returned to France in 1779–80 to get French aid for the United States. Back in America, he played a key role in the fighting in Virginia that climaxed in the Battle of Yorktown.

After the American Revolution, Lafayette returned again to France. He was an important figure during and after the French Revolution.

"The welfare of America is intimately bound up with the happiness of humanity. She is going to become a cherished and safe refuge of virtue, of good character, of tolerance, of equality and of a peaceful liberty."

Marquis de Lafayette, 1777

fortune of war has made me your prisoner." Gates replied, "I shall always be ready to testify that it was not through any fault of your excellency." The British surrendered a vast quantity of weapons, and the Redcoats were sent to a prison camp in Virginia.

The United States Gains Allies

The Americans' show of strength around Philadelphia and their victory at Saratoga marked a turning point in the war. It now appeared to the rest of the world that the United States might actually succeed in winning its independence from Britain.

From the earliest days of the Revolution, Congress had tried to get aid from abroad. France was eager to help. The French wanted to avenge their defeat by Britain in 1763. Months before news of the battles of October 1777 had reached Europe, France had promised some supplies. In the

Benjamin Franklin (1706–90)

Benjamin Franklin was one of the few Americans of his day to be an international celebrity. He was born in Boston, the tenth son in a family of 17 children. He became an apprentice to his older brother, a printer. At the age of 17, he moved first to New York and then to Philadelphia.

Franklin was an extremely versatile and talented man. Among other things, he ran a newspaper and became postmaster of the North American colonies. Franklin published *Poor Richard's Almanac*, a very popular magazine full of humor and useful advice.

Franklin was also an important scientist. His most famous experiment proved that lightning contained electricity. He made several other scientific discoveries, and also invented the lightning rod, bifocal eyeglasses, and the wood-burning stove that bears his name and is still being used today.

Through service in the Pennsylvania legislature, Franklin became a respected political leader. After the American Revolution, Franklin served as a member of the 1787 convention that wrote the U.S. Constitution. His last public act was to endorse a petition submitted to the U.S. Congress that called for ending the trade in slaves and action toward abolishing slavery.

Franklin is greeted at the French court of King Louis XVI.

fall of 1776, Benjamin Franklin took a delegation to France to seek a formal alliance and help in the war.

Franklin arrived in Paris on December 21, 1776. In his frontier-style fur cap, he delighted the French with his skill, wit, and charm. In early December 1777, news of Saratoga and Germantown reached Paris. King Louis XVI of France seemed ready to recognize American independence. On February 6, 1778, the Americans and French made a trade agreement and a treaty of alliance. France declared war on Britain and promised to supply the United States with money, equipment, a powerful navy, and thousands of troops.

Other European nations also supported the American cause. In 1779, Spain declared war on Britain and attacked British strongholds near the Gulf of Mexico. Spain, however, did not officially recognize American independence until after the Revolution. The Netherlands also went to war with Britain and lent money to the American cause.

The United States Navy

During the Revolution, Congress authorized many ships to be armed to fight for the Patriot cause. However, the United States had no official navy until 1794. The first ships built for the new U.S. Navy were frigates. These were small and fast warships built of wood and armed with around 40 guns. The United States Navy remained small, and it was about one hundred years before it began to compete with the great naval powers of Europe.

In 1907, the navy's "Great White Fleet" of 16 battleships set off on a world tour to show other nations how powerful the United States had become. In 1922, a treaty was signed between the world's five major naval powers. Britain, France, Italy, Japan, and the United States agreed to stop their race to build the greatest number of battleships. But by this time, the U.S. Navy already equaled the Royal Navy of Great Britain, which had dominated the seas for 250 years. And by the end of World War II, the United States Navy was by far the most powerful in the world. It remains so today.

5

The Revolution at Home

The years of American Revolution were a time when important changes were made. Many families and communities experienced great turmoil. There were difficult issues to decide. How would the former colonies, now states, govern themselves? How would the different groups of people in American society manage to live with each other?

Creating New State Governments

The main issue of the Revolutionary period was who would rule America. The states now had to change their existing governments, and in some cases create new ones.

After fighting began in 1775, the royal governors lost their authority, and most of them fled to Britain. By 1780, all 13 states had formally set up new governments. The colonial assemblies had been replaced by new governing bodies, usually with the same members as before.

Each state had a written constitution that explained the powers of its government. Most of these constitutions had a bill of rights. These stated the rights of the people, such as freedom of the press, the right of citizens to make requests to government, and the right to trial by jury. No permanent armies were allowed within the states, and people's property could not be searched without official permission. All state officials were to be chosen by the people, and no official positions could be passed from one person to another because of family or tradition. The government could not interfere with these rights.

> "All power is vested in, and consequently derived from, the people . . . magistrates are their trustees and servants, and at all times amenable to them."
>
> *Virginia Declaration of Rights*

57

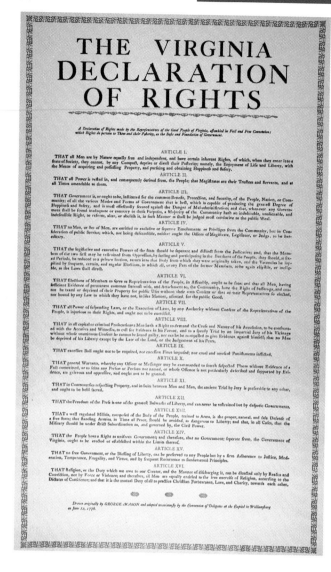

THE VIRGINIA
DECLARATION
OF RIGHTS

The Virginia Declaration of Rights was approved by Virginia's assembly in June 1776. It was the first of many written by the states to protect citizens from their own governments. Later, for the same reason, the Bill of Rights was added to the United States Constitution.

The legislature was the branch of government that made laws. This branch was closest to the people, and was given the most power. But Americans didn't want any branch of government to be too powerful. So every state (except Pennsylvania) divided its legislature into two bodies, or "houses." This way, the two houses could keep a check on each other.

The executive branch, which was the office of the governor, was made less powerful than the legislature. For a time, the state of Pennsylvania had no governor at all.

The Articles of Confederation

Even before independence was declared, Congress had begun to act as a national government for America. In June 1776, Congress appointed a committee to prepare a written constitution for the whole nation. The committee recommended a government very like the existing Congress.

The members of Congress considered the plan very carefully. How powerful should the national government be? How should it raise money? What powers, if any, should it be given by the states? Americans were fighting because they thought the British government had tried to take away their liberties. Now they wanted to make sure that their own government did not do the same thing. Congress completed its proposal for a new government in November 1777. The document was called the Articles of Confederation.

The Articles reflected what Americans saw as wrong in British government, and how they wanted to govern differently. They created a very limited national government, with only a legislative branch. No national courts were created.

The national government would be in charge of foreign relations, issuing money, and running the post office. It could not tax people, and it could only request money from the states. Each state would have one vote. Decisions would be made by majority vote on most matters, although some matters would have to be approved by at least nine states. Any changes to the Articles would have to be agreed to by all the states.

The Articles of Confederation did not go into effect until March 1, 1781. The delay was caused mainly by arguments over land. Several states had claims, some of them overlapping, to lands that stretched into the West. The other states said these claims should now belong to the whole nation. Eventually this was agreed upon, and the Articles were finally approved. The new national government kept the name Congress.

Raising Money

Because of their history under British rule, Americans were suspicious of national governments. This made it very hard for Congress to get the resources it needed to win the war.

Congress did not have the power to raise money itself. It depended on contributions from the states and from other countries. During the Revolutionary War, the states contributed about $5.8 million. Several more millions were borrowed from abroad, mostly from France. Congress also sold bonds to Americans. When they bought a bond, people were lending money to their country. The government promised to pay back the money, with an extra amount as interest on the loan, at a later date. More than $7 million in bonds were sold.

Too much paper money circulating during and after the Revolution caused the money to have little worth. The paper money seen here looked official, but it didn't buy much because few people trusted its value.

Both Congress and the states issued hundreds of millions of dollars worth of paper money. This money lost its value very quickly. The result was inflation—a rise in prices—as more and more money was needed to buy the same amount of goods. The inflation during the Revolution was the worst in American history. For example, in Maryland, a bag of salt cost $1 in 1776. A few years later, it cost $3,900!

The paper money Congress issued was known as "Continentals." Because of growing inflation, "not worth a Continental" became a common expression for something of little value. Congress was so short of money that it had great difficulty paying the salaries of the Continental Army's soldiers. On several occasions, there were mutinies in the army caused by delays in pay and poor supplies.

Life in Wartime

On the whole, the war did not greatly alter the social structure of America. But many people's lives were affected by it, and by the changes brought by the Revolution. Merchants were hurt when trade with Britain was cut off. While most merchants were Patriots, some wealthy ones were Loyalists. Many Loyalist merchants left America during the war.

Owners of large plantations in the South also suffered, as their crops of tobacco and rice could not be sold abroad. But on the whole, the wealthy plantation owners kept their wealth and their power. Some small farmers prospered, as their crops were sold to feed the armies.

When Loyalist landowners left because of the war, their estates were seized and sold. There was a curious situation in New York's Hudson valley. Landlords and tenants were usually on opposite sides during the war. When the wealthy Loyalist Frederick Philipse went into exile, nearly 300 former tenants divided up his land. The rich Livingston family, on the other hand, were Patriots. The Livingston tenants sided with the British. When General Burgoyne came south from Canada in the summer of 1777, these tenants clashed with Patriot militia.

For many individuals and families, the Revolution brought pain and suffering. Some of the Loyalists who left the country did so very reluctantly. Loyalists who stayed were often persecuted. Many states and communities had committees on the lookout for people who did not support the Patriot cause.

Most of the time, Loyalists were treated according to law. But the laws could be harsh. People who refused to swear allegiance to their new state governments could lose their rights as citizens. This meant they might lose their property and legal protection. They could not vote or hold office. Some Loyalists were prosecuted for treason, and a few were even executed.

Civilians as well as soldiers suffered in the violence of war. Towns and cities near battle sites were badly damaged. This happened to Charlestown, Massachusetts, in April 1775; to Norfolk, Virginia, in January 1776; and to Yorktown, Virginia, in October 1780. On several occasions, British

During the years of the Revolutionary War, home life was shattered for many by danger and death. The war was fought wherever British troops found resistance. Sometimes families, such as the one seen below, had to defend their homes against attack.

American Cities under British Occupation

Several American cities were under British control during the Revolution. The British occupied New York City for seven years, from 1776 to 1783. Boston, Philadelphia, Savannah, and Charleston were also occupied for long periods.

Life was often hard for people in these cities. In Boston, fresh food became scarce, as the Patriot forces blocked off roads to the surrounding farms. British soldiers tore down buildings to provide themselves with firewood. Officers took over private homes for their residences. General Clinton, for example, took over the home of Patriot leader John Hancock.

Philadelphia suffered less because it was not hemmed in by another, opposing army. But soldiers still stole from civilians and made them uncomfortable. Meanwhile, British officers and wealthy Loyalists enjoyed an active social season with plays, concerts, and weekly balls. One young woman wrote, "You can have no idea of the life of continued amusement I live. . . . There is a ball every Thursday, never a lack of partners, for you must know 'tis a fixed rule never to dance but two dances at a time with the same person. . . . I am engaged to seven different gentlemen."

New York also had a busy cultural scene. But it also had a severe housing shortage. As many as 10,000 British troops and many thousands of Loyalists had come to the city. And the fire during the 1776 fighting had burned about 500 homes in New York, one-quarter of the total.

When the British finally left the occupied cities, thousands of Loyalists went with them. In Savannah and Charleston, thousands of runaway slaves also left with the Redcoats.

raiders terrorized Connecticut towns. In July 1779, more than 200 houses in Fairfield were burned, and Norwalk was torched. In September 1781, most of New London was destroyed.

As British and American armies tramped back and forth across the countryside, they stole crops, tore down fences and farm buildings for firewood, and often robbed homes. Generals on both side punished these actions, but could not prevent them.

Women in the Revolution

Soldiers and their loved ones back home missed each other. Women were left at home while their fathers, husbands, or sons went to war. They had to endure loneliness and anxiety over whether their men would ever return.

During the war, some women did work that was usually done by men. John Adams's wife, Abigail, managed the family farm, as did many other women throughout America. Esther Reed of Philadelphia was the wife of a member of Washington's staff. She organized a committee that raised money to help supply the Continental Army. After Reed died in 1780, Benjamin Franklin's daughter Sarah continued her work. Women wove cloth for soldiers' clothing and blankets. Mercy Otis Warren of Massachusetts, the sister of the lawyer James Otis, wrote plays and essays supporting the Patriot cause.

"I look for you almost every day but I don't allow myself to depend on any thing for I find there is nothing to be depended upon but trouble and disappointments. . . . I want to see you.

I have got a Sweet babe almost six months old but have got no father for it . . . . All I can do for you is to commit you to God . . . for God is as able to preserve us as ever and he will do it if we trust in him aright."

Letters from Sarah Hodgkins to her husband Joseph Hodgkins, a soldier in the Massachusetts militia

Like other women all over the former colonies, this group in Philadelphia made clothes for the Continental Army.

Molly Pitcher at the battlefront.

Women on the Front Lines

During the Revolutionary War, some women took part in the fighting. Margaret Corbin was born in western Pennsylvania in 1751. When she was only four, her father was killed and her mother kidnapped by Indians. Corbin remained with her husband when he joined the Continental Army. After he was killed at Fort Washington, New York, in 1776, she took his place and was herself wounded. In 1779, Congress awarded Corbin half pay for life.

Another legendary woman was Molly Pitcher. Her real name was probably Mary Ludwig Hays. Born in 1754 in Carlisle, Pennsylvania, she accompanied her husband, John Hays, after he enlisted in the Continental Army. She washed, cooked, and nursed for the troops. According to one account, Pitcher "smoked, chewed tobacco, and swore like a trooper." She was carrying water to the front lines at the Battle of Monmouth on June 28, 1778, when her husband was wounded while loading a cannon. Molly Pitcher simply stepped in and continued his work.

Deborah Sampson disguised herself as a man so she could be a soldier. Born in Massachusetts in 1760, she enlisted as "Robert Shurtliff." Sampson was wounded several times but tended her wounds herself so she would not be discovered. Eventually she was found out when she became sick. When Sampson died in 1827, her husband received a government pension as a war "widow."

Blacks and the Revolution

When the Revolution began, about 400,000 black people lived in America. More than 90 percent of these blacks were slaves. Slaves lived in every colony, but the overwhelming majority of them were in the South.

There were about 50,000 blacks who were not slaves. These people were called "free blacks." Free blacks lived in nearly equal numbers in North and South. Nowhere, however, did they enjoy the rights of white people. They were restricted in everything they did. White people decided where they made their homes, what kind of education they could have, and how they could earn their livings.

Many of the most important leaders of the Revolution thought slavery was wrong. But not all Revolutionary leaders opposed slavery, and even those who did were often slave owners themselves. George Washington and Thomas Jefferson, for example, owned many slaves.

Black people took part in the war on both sides. As many as 5,000 blacks fought on the Patriot side. They were present in almost every major battle, from Lexington in 1775 to Yorktown in 1781. There were black men among Vermont's militia, the Green Mountain Boys, and on board warships.

Some slaves fought in the war to gain their freedom. Some became soldiers as a way of escaping from slavery. Others were sent to fight by their masters. Free blacks had the same variety of reasons for fighting as whites did. They may have believed in the cause, or they may have wanted the money or land they were promised for serving as soldiers.

Many whites in southern states were uneasy about giving guns to black people, and allowing them to serve as soldiers. The whites were fearful of slave revolts. For this reason, Congress and the Continental Army discouraged blacks from enlisting at the beginning of the war. But that policy soon changed. The Continental Army became the most integrated army in America's history until very recently. Usually, blacks and whites served side by side. However, Rhode Island had an all-black regiment commanded by white officers.

"In the woods [we saw] herds of Negroes which [British General Cornwallis] . . . had turned adrift, with no other recompense for their confidence in his humanity than the smallpox for their bounty and starvation and death for their wages. They might be seen scattered about in every direction, dead and dying, with pieces of ears of burnt Indian corn in the hands and mouths."

Joseph Plumb Martin, a soldier at Yorktown, 1781

James Lafayette (17?–18?)

James Lafayette was a slave who spied on the British for the Americans. Nobody knows when he was born or died, but there are paintings of him. He belonged to William Armistead of Virginia. Until his service in the Revolution, he was known as James Armistead, as slaves were usually given their owners' last names.

In 1781, with his owner's approval, James volunteered to spy for the American forces in Virginia led by the Marquis de Lafayette. He was very useful because he could move freely in and out of the British lines. Lafayette praised James's

James Lafayette with the Marquis de Lafayette.

work, and after the war James was given his freedom. The state paid James's owner the current price for an adult male slave.

As a free man, James took the last name "Lafayette." In 1819, Virginia granted him an annual pension. When the Marquis de Lafayette made a last, grand tour of America in 1824, James Lafayette was there to greet him.

Black people also fought on the British side. Lord Dunmore, the royal governor of Virginia, had proclaimed that all slaves who joined the British would be freed. Some of the blacks who answered his call ended up as free men in Canada. Others settled in the British colony of Sierra Leone in Africa. Still others simply ran away in the confusion of war.

British officials did not appeal for black soldiers again until years later, when they were desperate for troops. During the fighting in the Carolinas, thousands of blacks joined the British army. In 1781, 17 of Washington's slaves fled from Mount Vernon to a British ship. The black soldiers who joined the British were not always well treated. Many were packed into camps where smallpox and other diseases killed large numbers.

Some Patriots realized that the existence of slavery in America contradicted their ideals of freedom and liberty. During the Revolution, efforts were made to end slavery. In 1778, for example, Governor William Livingston of New Jersey asked the legislature to free all the slaves in the state. In some places, blacks argued on their own behalf. In New Hampshire, slaves petitioned the legislature for their freedom so "that the name of slave may not more be heard in a land gloriously contending for the sweets of freedom."

During and just after the Revolution, many states outside the South did pass laws that provided for the gradual ending of slavery. Unfortunately, this did not result in great numbers of freed slaves, as most were sold to plantation owners in the southern states. But even in the South, several states changed their laws to make it easier to free slaves. To many Patriots, the Revolution did seem to be bringing nearer the day when slavery would be ended in America.

> "[Slavery is] utterly inconsistent with the principles of Christianity and humanity; and in Americans who have idolized liberty, peculiarly odious and disgraceful."
>
> *William Livingston, governor of New Jersey*

People Power

At the time of the American Revolution, only very few people had the right to vote for their governments. In all the states, people had to own property in order to vote. Voters had to be white and, in most cases, male. Before independence, a few colonies had allowed female property owners to vote also. But after the Declaration of Independence, New Jersey was the only state that continued to let some women vote.

Over the years, the right to vote was extended. More white male citizens became eligible to vote. In 1870, the Fifteenth Amendment to the Constitution guaranteed the vote to all male citizens, regardless of their "race, color, or previous condition of servitude." In practice, however, black men were still stopped from voting in many states. It was not until 1920, with the Nineteenth Amendment, that women all over the United States were given the right to vote. And it took the Civil Rights Acts of the 1960s to ensure a vote for every black person. Since 1971, all citizens of 18 years or older (except convicted criminals and mentally ill people) have been allowed to vote.

6

The War Continues

Word of the alliance with France did not reach America until the spring of 1778. French aid took even longer to arrive. Meanwhile, Washington and the main part of his army suffered through the bitter winter of 1777–78 at Valley Forge, Pennsylvania. In Philadelphia, 21 miles (34 km) away, the British were enjoying the comforts of the city.

Valley Forge and Monmouth

Valley Forge was a village on the west bank of the Schuylkill River. The river and steep hillsides helped protect the field where the army made camp. But the troops were short of the most basic requirements: decent food, clothing, and shelter.

Local farmers wouldn't sell their crops for Congress's worthless paper money. Instead, they sent their produce to Philadelphia, where the British paid in gold and silver. In desperation, Washington told soldiers to seize food from the farms that had refused to sell.

Early in 1778, Washington reported to Congress that he had nearly 3,000 men "unfit for duty, because barefoot and other wise naked." He said there were "4,000 men wanting blankets, near 2,000 of which have never had one, altho' some of them have been 12 months in service." By the end of the winter, about 2,500 had died from the bad conditions. Another thousand deserted.

Washington told the troops that he would share their hardships. His Christmas dinner, served in a tent, had neither, bread, sugar, tea, coffee, nor milk. He lived in a tent until housing had been built for his men. About 900 small,

"Our brave fellows [are] living in tents bare-footed, bare-legged, bare-breeched . . . in snow, in rain, on marches, in camp, and on duty. Nothing but virtue has kept our army together."

Colonel John Brooks of the Continental Army

windowless huts were built. Twelve men squeezed into each hut, sleeping on wooden bunks or on straw mats.

Somehow, the army survived through the winter, and slowly things improved. Wives of the officers, including Martha Washington, made clothes and helped care for the sick. New recruits arrived in spring, along with clothing and other supplies.

During their time at Valley Forge, the Continental Army was trained by Friedrich Wilhelm von Steuben, a Prussian officer. Von Steuben had fought in Europe under Frederick the Great. His strict drilling soon made the army into a more effective fighting force. On March 24, 1778, the army put on a demonstration drill showing its improved discipline and spirit.

On May 3, 1778, word arrived at Valley Forge of the alliance with France. Three days later, the army formally celebrated. There was a morning prayer, then a parade and

George Washington visits sick soldiers at Valley Forge. In the unusually cold winter of 1777–78, Washington's men were weak from disease and near starvation. At one point, a third of them had no shoes or leggings, and half had no blankets. Some soldiers had no clothes except rags.

Joseph Plumb Martin (1760–1850)

Joseph Plumb Martin, an ordinary soldier, was the author of one of the best memoirs of the American Revolution.

Martin was the son of a preacher. He was self-educated and raised by his grandparents in Milford, Connecticut. In 1776, Martin enlisted in the Connecticut militia at the age of 15. The next year, he joined the Continental Army and served for the remainder of the war. He carried with him a small box containing a lock of his girlfriend's hair.

Martin fought in the battles around New York City and suffered through the winter of 1777–78 at Valley Forge. He was home on leave in 1781 when the army suddenly moved south to Virginia. Martin walked 400 miles (644 km) to join his comrades. He then took part in the crucial battle of Yorktown. By that time, he had risen from private to sergeant.

After the war, Martin led an ordinary life. He wrote about his war experiences when he was in his seventies.

a firing of arms. The men cheered "Long live the king of France! Long live the American States!" Washington played the British game of cricket with his aides.

It was fortunate for the Continental Army that the British under Sir William Howe attacked very little during the winter at Valley Forge. Fearful of being trapped by a French fleet, the British left Philadelphia in June 1778 and headed for New York. About 9,000 Redcoats were accompanied by 3,000 Loyalist civilians. They went by land, traveling with 1,500 wagons. In a column stretching for 12 miles (19 km), they made slow progress. Patriots in New Jersey wrecked bridges along their path. In return, the British cut down fruit trees and killed farm animals.

Washington chased after the British. Advance troops under General Lee attacked the British at Monmouth, New Jersey, on June 28. It was a blisteringly hot day. Many soldiers were felled by sunstroke. The Patriots were doing well until General Lee suddenly ordered a retreat. There was confusion in the ranks and the British were able to drive the Patriots back. Washington arrived at the scene, furious with Lee. He rallied his troops and the battle continued all day. At night, the British fled to New York. The Americans then established posts around the city.

Monmouth turned out to be the last major battle of the war in the North. In 1779, there were some small battles in the Hudson Highlands in New York State.

Benedict Arnold's Treason

Benedict Arnold was a brave military officer who had served the Patriot cause well. But he became the most notorious traitor in American history.

The Continental Army built a fort at West Point, about 50 miles (80 km) from New York City. Washington made Arnold commander of West Point, but Arnold was already in secret contact with the British. He made a deal to turn West Point over to them for money. The British major John André came to West Point on the night of September 22, 1780, to settle plans with Arnold. But on his way back to New York, André was captured and the plot revealed. Arnold managed to escape to British lines.

Native Americans and Northwest Forts

In the 1700s, parts of the frontier were still only a few hundred miles from the Atlantic Ocean. Western New York State and northern and western Pennsylvania, for example, were still frontier areas, as were the western regions of all the southern states. In 1776, Georgia, the Carolinas, and Virginia sent 6,000 men to their frontiers to fight the Cherokee Indians, who had sided with the British.

The British maintained several forts in the area called the "Northwest." (See map on page 75.) This was the region between the Ohio and Mississippi Rivers and the Great Lakes. From their forts, the British encouraged Indian raids on American settlements. An estimated 13,000 Native Americans fought with the British during the Revolution.

Very bloody clashes took place in the Wyoming Valley in northern Pennsylvania and in the Cherry Valley west of Albany, New York. About 400 Loyalists and 500 Seneca and Delaware Indians marched 200 miles (321 km) south from Fort Niagara to attack the Wyoming Valley in July 1778. Hundreds of people, both Native American and white, were scalped and about 1,000 homes destroyed. In November of the same year, hundreds of Loyalists and Iroquois Indians, led by the Mohawk chief Joseph Brant, terrorized the Cherry Valley.

"The enemy killed, scalped and most barbarously murdered thirty-two inhabitants, chiefly women and children. . . . [They] committed the most inhuman barbarities on most of the dead."

New Jersey Gazette, 1778

At Congress's request, Washington ordered General John Sullivan to retaliate for these attacks. In July 1779, Sullivan led 4,000 men against Native Americans in New York and Pennsylvania. The Iroquois lived in stone or wooden houses surrounded by cultivated fields and orchards. Sullivan followed his instructions to take many Indian hostages, "ruin" their crops, and see that their settlements were "not merely overrun but destroyed."

The main British base in the Northwest was Fort Detroit, commanded by Henry Hamilton. Hamilton was called the "hair buyer" because he was believed to offer payments to Indians for settlers' scalps.

American settlements in the Ohio Valley were repeatedly attacked. Major George Rogers Clark was sent to end these attacks. In June 1778, Clark and about 200 men sailed down the Ohio River to the mouth of the Tennessee River. They then marched 120 miles (193 km) overland to Kaskaskia in what is now Illinois. After taking it and other British outposts, they captured the larger town of Vincennes, now in Indiana.

While Clark was away at Kaskaskia in December, Hamilton retook Vincennes for the British. Clark vowed to get it back. In February 1779, he and his men marched for days, at times through shoulder-deep, icy water, to surprise the British. Hamilton surrendered but Clark never achieved his aim of capturing Detroit. At the end of the war, Clark's exploits helped the United States' claim to the Northwest in the peace settlement.

The War at Sea

At the start of the Revolution, America had no official navy, although there were many merchant ships that could be armed and used in the fighting. The British navy, on the other hand, was the largest in the world. Britain was able to send dozens of warships to blockade ports up and down the American coast. Fast American vessels could sometimes slip by the warships, but at first Britain controlled almost everything going in and out of the main harbors of the United States.

Joseph Brant (1742–1807) was the most important Indian leader in the American Revolution. He persuaded many Iroquois tribes to support the British, who made him a captain.

From October 1775, Congress ordered 13 warships to be built. Most of these, however, never got to sea or were quickly captured by the British. Several states also built tiny navies of their own.

American privateers were more successful. A privateer was a ship formerly used for trade that was armed to attack British shipping. Congress authorized hundreds of ships to sail as privateers. France allowed American privateers to take shelter in its ports.

John Paul Jones was one of the boldest commanders of the privateers. In 1776, he captured eight vessels in 49 days. During 1777 and 1778, Jones raided the coasts and ports of the British Isles.

In August 1779, Jones took over an old French ship. He renamed it the *Bonhomme Richard*, French for "Poor Richard." This was in honor of Benjamin Franklin's *Poor Richard's Almanac.* On September 23, 1779, Jones and his ship took part in one of the most exciting naval battles in American history.

Jones was sailing near Flamborough Head on the east coast of Great Britain. He came upon a large fleet of merchant ships escorted by the British warship *Serapis.* The *Bonhomme Richard* attacked the *Serapis* at close quarters, and the two ships fought for four hours. The decks of both ships were littered with dead bodies. At one point, Jones's ship was so badly damaged that the British captain asked Jones whether he wished to surrender. Jones supposedly replied, "I have not yet begun to fight." In the end, it was the *Serapis* that surrendered, although the *Bonhomme Richard* sank the next day.

The Serapis *was a large, new warship with more guns on board than the* Bonhomme Richard. *But heavy firing by Jones's men forced the British eventually to surrender. The American crew abandoned the damaged* Bonhomme Richard, *and sailed into port on the* Serapis.

The War in the South

There had been little fighting in the South since 1776. But now the British began to look on the South as a more promising place for military action. They believed there were many Loyalists in the area, especially in North and South Carolina and in Georgia. With Loyalist help, the British thought they could capture and hold large areas. These would serve as bases from which to move northward and convince the Patriots to end the Revolution.

Early in 1778, General Sir Henry Clinton had taken over from Howe as the British commander in chief. In the fall, he sent 3,500 troops from New York to attack Savannah, Georgia. Together with another 2,000 men coming up from Florida, the Redcoats surprised the Patriot defenders in December. They inflicted many casualties while suffering very few. After capturing Augusta a month later, the British controlled Georgia. In October 1779, the Americans and their French allies tried without success to retake Savannah.

In early 1780, Clinton left a small force in New York and came south with a large army to attack Charleston. The city was defended by Patriots led by General Benjamin Lincoln, but its defenses were not as strong as they had been in 1776. The British outnumbered the Patriots by 11,500 to 5,500. Many farmers and plantation owners refused to leave their lands and help the defense because they feared slave revolts.

Charleston is on a peninsula. The water around it was controlled by the British. In late March, they seized the land approach as well and began a siege. In April, they started a bombardment. On May 12, Lincoln surrendered, and the entire Patriot army was taken prisoner. It was the worst American defeat of the war.

Clinton returned to New York and left Lord Cornwallis in charge of the South. Cornwallis began a campaign to secure the Carolinas. In June 1780, General Horatio Gates, the victor at Saratoga, took command of all the American forces in the South. After a long march, his army of 7,000 men attacked Cornwallis's force at Camden, South Carolina,

"We look on America as at our feet."

A member of British Parliament, after the capture of Charleston

on August 16. The attack failed. The Patriot army fell apart, and General Gates hurried from the scene ahead of his retreating men.

The British seemed unbeatable in the South. But as their troops moved through the countryside, their supply lines and communications were often attacked by small forces of local Patriots. These bands would appear suddenly, strike their blows, and then disappear before a regular battle could be fought. This kind of fighting is called "guerrilla warfare." One of the best guerrilla leaders was Frances Marion, who was based in the swamps of eastern South Carolina. He became known as the "Swamp Fox."

There was bitter fighting between Loyalists and Patriots in the Carolinas. A Loyalist army of about 1,100, led by Major Patrick Ferguson, invaded central North Carolina.

From 1778 to 1781, the war of the American Revolution spread to the Northwest and into the South.

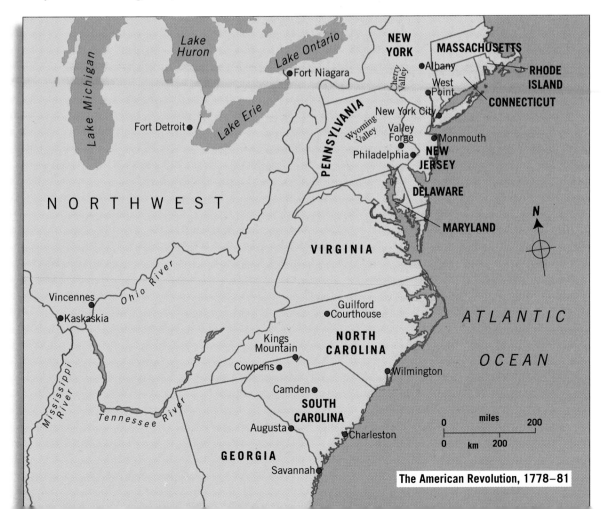

The American Revolution, 1778–81

> "We fight, get beat, rise and fight again."
>
> *Nathanael Greene, 1781*

> "I am quite tired of marching about the country. . . . If we mean an offensive war in America, we must abandon New York and bring our whole force into Virginia."
>
> *General Cornwallis, April 1781*

On October 6, 1780, the Loyalists faced a force of Patriot frontier riflemen at Kings Mountain. Ferguson announced that he "defied God Almighty and all the rebels out of hell to overcome him." But he was killed and his army destroyed.

In October, Washington persuaded Congress to send Nathanael Greene to replace Gates in the South. Greene fought Cornwallis again and again. He won few outright victories, but managed to exhaust the British and cause them heavy losses. In January 1781, at Cowpens in South Carolina, one of Greene's units did defeat the British. Greene then fought a fierce battle with Cornwallis at Guilford Courthouse, North Carolina, on March 15.

After this, Cornwallis had to withdraw 150 miles (241 km) to Wilmington for supplies. Without consulting Clinton, he then decided to leave the Carolinas and march his army up to Virginia. Clinton thought the move "inexcusable." Greene stayed in the Carolinas, battling the British at posts on the rivers. By autumn, the British had lost their hold on the South. They were secure only in Charleston and Savannah.

The Revolution Happened Here

All over the eastern United States, there are places packed with the history of the American Revolution. The city of Boston has several sites which are linked together in a "Freedom Trail" that people can follow around the city. The site of the Boston Massacre, Paul Revere's house, and the Battle of Bunker Hill memorial are all on the route.

Also in Massachusetts are the battlefields of Lexington and Concord, where the Revolutionary War began. Other preserved battlefields include Cowpens in South Carolina; and Yorktown, Virginia, where the final battle for America was fought in October 1781.

Valley Forge, the Continental Army's camp in Pennsylvania, is now a historical park. Visitors can see where soldiers lived through the freezing winter of 1777 to 1778. The soldiers' huts, the officers' houses, and even George Washington's field tent all conjure up army life during the American Revolution.

America Wins Its Independence

B y spring 1781, the war of the American Revolution had been going on for six years. No end was in sight, and both sides were in low spirits.

The Situation in Early 1781

In 1781, the British occupied New York City, Charleston, and Savannah. They also had armies in Virginia. But they were no closer than ever to ending the American rebellion against their rule. From New York, Sir Henry Clinton wrote to the British government in London of "the utter impossibility of prosecuting the war in this country without reinforcements." Clinton claimed he needed thousands more troops "to subdue this formidable rebellion."

In January 1781, Pennsylvania troops killed an officer in New Jersey during a protest over lack of pay. They then marched to Philadelphia to demand their money from Congress.

The Americans were worried, too. Washington and the main force of the Continental Army—only about 3,500 men at this time—were camped on the Hudson River north of New York City. The army was short of food, clothing, and ammunition. The soldiers had not been paid, since Congress had no money. No new men were joining, and there had been mutinies.

77

> "We are at the end of our tether and now or never our deliverance must come."
>
> *George Washington, April 1781*

The aid from France had not produced many benefits. Over 4,000 French soldiers had landed at Rhode Island in 1780, but they had seen little fighting. A promised second division had not arrived, and most of the French fleet had already left America. Congress and Washington appealed to France for more help.

The British Fall into a Trap

Benedict Arnold, who had now joined the British side, was in Virginia with more than 3,000 Redcoats. Their orders were to cause as much destruction as possible. Washington sent the Marquis de Lafayette with 1,200 men to try and stop them. Lafayette got to Virginia in April 1781. Soon other troops arrived, led by General Anthony Wayne, increasing the American forces to 5,000.

On May 20, 1781, Lord Cornwallis arrived with his army at Petersburg, Virginia. He took charge of all the British troops in the state, and his 7,000 men outnumbered the Americans. Pretty much all Lafayette could do was keep his distance and watch the British movements.

In June, one of Cornwallis's officers, Banastre Tarleton, raided Charlottesville, which was then Virginia's capital. Tarleton captured seven Virginia legislators and came within minutes of seizing the governor, Thomas Jefferson.

Clinton ordered Cornwallis to establish a position near Chesapeake Bay. There he could receive a large fleet as well as prepare land operations. Cornwallis chose as his base the village of Yorktown, on the York Peninsula between the mouths of the James and York Rivers. Yorktown is on a bluff overlooking the York River. The land in front of the town is flat, offering no military advantages to anyone defending it.

Cornwallis and his army arrived at Yorktown early in August and began building fortifications around the town and on Gloucester Point, directly across the river. Following Cornwallis cautiously, Lafayette moved the American troops near Williamsburg, 7 miles (11 km) up the peninsula. He now saw the possibility of trapping the British on the peninsula.

Washington also had been watching the situation. He and the leader of the French army in America, Count de Rochambeau, met in Connecticut to discuss a joint operation against the British. Rochambeau gave Washington the very welcome news that France was sending a large fleet, commanded by Admiral François de Grasse, to help America. In June, the French army marched from its base at Newport to join the Americans camped on the Hudson River.

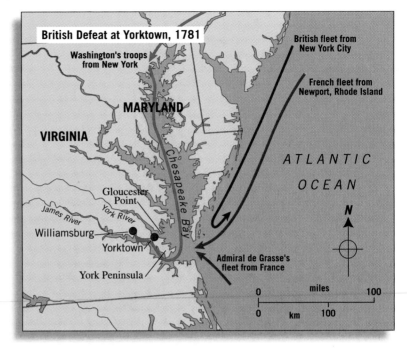

British Defeat at Yorktown, 1781

Washington's troops from New York

MARYLAND

VIRGINIA

Chesapeake Bay

James River

York River

Gloucester Point

Williamsburg

Yorktown

York Peninsula

British fleet from New York City

French fleet from Newport, Rhode Island

ATLANTIC OCEAN

N

Admiral de Grasse's fleet from France

miles 100

km 100

Washington's first thought was to attack the British in New York City. But he and Rochambeau soon agreed they would not be able to defeat the 15,000 troops Clinton had there. Then, in August, Washington learned that Admiral de Grasse was on his way to Chesapeake Bay with a large fleet of warships and 3,000 soldiers. The fleet would only stay until October 14. Washington and Rochambeau made a bold plan: They would hurry south to join Lafayette. With the aid of the French fleet, they would then trap Cornwallis's army.

The plan was a great gamble. Yorktown was 450 miles (724 km) away. The American and French armies would have to go much of the way on foot and then sail down Chesapeake Bay. Food, tents, and boats were all needed. Their heavy guns would go by sea, on board a small French fleet sailing from Newport. But what if Clinton's large army blocked the route? What if a British fleet stopped de Grasse's fleet or the ships from Newport? What if Cornwallis managed to defeat Lafayette and leave Yorktown before the Americans and French could get there?

With the French fleets gaining control of the water around Yorktown, and Washington's forces arriving from the north, the Patriots had the British army trapped.

"[The American army was] composed of men of every age, even of children of fifteen, whites and blacks, almost naked, unpaid, and rather poorly fed."

A French officer, arriving at the American camp, New York, June 1781

Washington left a small part of his army on the Hudson. The main force and the entire French force started moving south the last week in August. For a few critical weeks, Clinton was fooled into thinking this move was directed against New York. When he realized what was happening, Clinton wrote Cornwallis that Washington was heading south, and promised to send reinforcements.

On September 5, Washington received very good news. The French fleet had reached Chesapeake Bay, and was near to Yorktown. Washington and Rochambeau reached Williamsburg on September 14, where they met Lafayette and his troops. By September 26, all the American and French forces had arrived. The French fleet had driven off a British fleet that had sailed down from New York. Talking about Cornwallis's situation, General Anthony Wayne told Lafayette, "Every door is shut."

The Siege of Yorktown

Cornwallis had about 10,000 men including British troops, Hessians, and about 100 Loyalists. The Americans and French far outnumbered them and had more artillery. Altogether, Washington had about 20,000 men—11,000 Americans and 9,000 French—under his command. Many men on both sides, however, were sick with malaria and other fevers.

At dawn on September 28, the Americans and French began moving out of Williamsburg toward Yorktown. They, like the British, built extensive fortifications. Their plan was to besiege Yorktown and bombard the British into surrendering. They would also besiege the British position on Gloucester Point (see map on page 79).

The bombardment began in the afternoon of October 9, 1781. A few days later, American and French troops stormed and overran a number of British positions. Now their gun batteries were even closer to Yorktown. The bombardment was terribly effective, heavier than anything the British had so far experienced in the war.

"The present moment will decide American independence. . . . The liberties of America and the honour of the Allied Armies are in our hands."

Washington to troops at Yorktown, September 30, 1781

On October 15, Cornwallis wrote Clinton that his condition was "very critical." That night, he ordered an attack on some of the gun batteries that had been pounding the British lines. It did little good, and the next day he tried a desperate move. Around midnight, 1,000 British soldiers boarded boats to cross the York River. The plan was to land on Gloucester Point, break through the encirclement there, and escape into the countryside. The sick and wounded, the heavy guns, and the horses would all be left behind in Yorktown. But luck was against the British. That night, a storm arose and wrecked the attempted escape. The few men who made it across the river returned the next day. They reported, "We'll never break through there. . . . Nothing passes in or out."

When the bombardment of Yorktown began on October 9, 1781, Washington fired the first American gun.

The British Surrender

On October 17, the American and French bombardment was heavier than ever. Only about 3,200 British soldiers were still fit for service. After an early morning inspection, Cornwallis met with his staff. He decided his situation was hopeless, and that it was time to give up.

The next day, the British asked for a cease-fire. Surrender talks went on all day and into the night. An agreement was reached the next morning. All troops would surrender themselves and their weapons. But the officers could keep their personal arms and were free to return home.

The formal surrender ceremony took place that afternoon on a field in front of Yorktown. It was an impressive sight. The American troops lined up on one side with Washington at the head. The French were on the other side headed by

Washington insepcts the French (left) and American (right) soldiers at the surrender ceremony on October 19, 1781. When the British surrendered, they marched in a long line between the French and American troops.

Rochambeau. While they waited for the British, a French military band played lively tunes.

The two armies looked strikingly different. The French were elegant in handsome white and gray uniforms with colored collars. Washington and some of his officers wore the yellow and blue of the Virginia militia that had become the official American uniform in 1779. But many American soldiers had no uniforms at all.

At last, about half of the British army appeared. The rest of the men were sick or wounded. The infantry wore their famous red coats, and the artillerymen wore blue. Cornwallis himself did not appear. His second-in-command tried to surrender to Washington but was told to hand over his sword to General Lincoln, Washington's second. Then the British army passed between the French and Americans, laying down their weapons. The French band played more tunes, including Yankee Doodle. The British surrendered thousands of muskets, and hundreds of artillery pieces and horses. Two days later, the thousands of British prisoners were marched off to camps in Virginia and Maryland.

Casualties at Yorktown were relatively light. The British lost 156 men killed, 326 wounded, and 70 missing. The Americans suffered only 3 killed and 65 wounded. The French lost 60 killed and 134 wounded. The 7,000 captured men were about one-quarter of all the British troops in America.

On the very day of the surrender, Sir Henry Clinton and thousands of British troops had set sail from New York to come to Cornwallis's aid. It was, of course, too late. They did not arrive in Chesapeake Bay until October 24. When Clinton learned what had happened, he ordered the ships to turn around and head back to New York.

> "Oh God! Oh God! It is all over! It is all over!"
>
> *The British Prime Minister Lord North on hearing of the British surrender at Yorktown*

Victory for the United States

Yorktown was the last major battle of the American Revolution, although not the very end of the fighting. The British still held the cities of Wilmington in North Carolina, Charleston in South Carolina, Savannah in Georgia, and New York. Expecting the war to last another year, Washington sent reinforcements to Greene in the Carolinas. The bulk of the Continental Army returned north to the New York area. Rochambeau remained near Yorktown with the French army. More clashes took place on the frontier.

But when news of the outcome at Yorktown reached the British government on November 25, the result was dramatic. In Parliament, support for the war in America had been declining for some time. Now the British had had enough. Late in February 1782, Parliament passed a motion declaring that the war "be no longer pursued." King George III stubbornly wished to continue the fight. In the end, however, he appointed new ministers who accepted American independence.

Formal peace talks began in Paris in September 1782. After much negotiation, Britain and the United States came to an agreement. The final Treaty of Paris was signed on September 3, 1783. Congress ratified the Treaty on January 14, 1784. In the meantime, the British had also made peace with France, Spain, and the Netherlands.

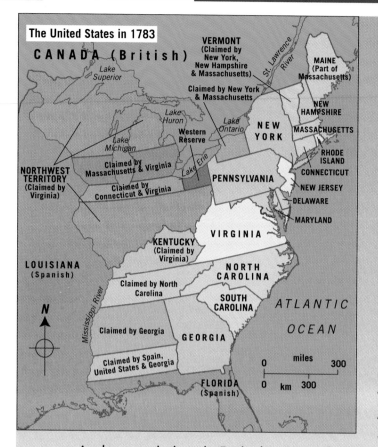

The United States in 1783

CANADA (British)

Lake Superior

VERMONT
(Claimed by New York, New Hampshire & Massachusetts)

MAINE
(Part of Massachusetts)

St. Lawrence River

Claimed by New York & Massachusetts

Lake Huron

Lake Michigan

Western Reserve

Lake Ontario

NEW YORK

NEW HAMPSHIRE

MASSACHUSETTS

Claimed by Massachusetts & Virginia

NORTHWEST TERRITORY
(Claimed by Virginia)

Claimed by Connecticut & Virginia

Lake Erie

PENNSYLVANIA

RHODE ISLAND

CONNECTICUT

NEW JERSEY

DELAWARE

MARYLAND

VIRGINIA

KENTUCKY
(Claimed by Virginia)

LOUISIANA
(Spanish)

Claimed by North Carolina

NORTH CAROLINA

Mississippi River

N

Claimed by Georgia

SOUTH CAROLINA

GEORGIA

ATLANTIC OCEAN

Claimed by Spain, United States & Georgia

FLORIDA
(Spanish)

| 0 | miles | 300 |
| 0 | km | 300 |

The Treaty of Paris

Before the Treaty of Paris, there had already been attempts at negotiating peace. In September 1776, an unsuccessful peace conference took place on Staten Island. The talks were polite, but they failed because the British would not recognize American independence. Two years later, shaken by America's alliance with France, the British again proposed to end the war. They still would not recognize American independence, and Congress refused.

At the negotiations in Paris that started in September 1782, the Americans made four major demands on Britain:

1. that it recognize the independence of the United States;
2. that the Mississippi River form the United States' western border, with Americans having the right to use the river;
3. that the Great Lakes form the boundary with Canada;
4. that Americans have the right to fish at the Grand Banks off Newfoundland.

In October 1782, the British accepted these four conditions. All in all, the Treaty was a triumph for the new, independent United States of America. The nation would extend from Canada to Florida (which Britain gave back to Spain), and from the Atlantic Ocean to the Mississippi River. This was more territory than the United States had controlled at the end of the war. All British armed forces were to leave American territory.

News of the agreement had reached the United States in March 1783, before the formal signing. The British pulled out of New York City on November 25. That same day, George Washington entered the city. On December 4, he made a tearful farewell to his officers at Fraunces Tavern in lower Manhattan. Earlier, he had firmly rejected suggestions by some officers that he become king of America. A few weeks later, in an emotional ceremony, Washington resigned from the army at a meeting of Congress in Annapolis, Maryland. He presented his sword to Congress. This was to show that, in the United States, the power of Congress, and therefore the people, should always be stronger than that of the military. Washington returned home to Mount Vernon in time for Christmas.

"Having now finished the work assigned me I retire from the great theatre of action, and bidding an affectionate farewell to this august body under whose orders I have so long acted, I here offer my commission and take my leave of all the employments of public life."

George Washington to Congress, December 23, 1783

John Jay (standing, left), John Adams (seated, left), Benjamin Franklin (seated, center), and Henry Laurens (standing, center) were the main negotiators for the United States at the Treaty of Paris. Franklin was accompanied by his grandson (seated, right). The British delegates refused to sit for this painting, which is why it is unfinished.

Stars and Stripes

After the Declaration of Independence, Congress decided on a new flag for the United States. It would have 13 red and white stripes to stand for the 13 states. The upper left corner, called the canton, would be blue with 13 white stars. This pattern was interpreted in many different ways, and a variety of flags were flown during the Revolution, first at sea and later in land battles.

In 1795, another Flag Act was passed in Congress. By this time, there were two new states, and so the flag would now have 15 stars and 15 stripes. However, there were five more states by 1817 that were not represented on the flag. Congress agreed that from now on, the number of stars would increase every time a new state was admitted to the union. The stripes would be reduced back to 13, to represent the original states.

The national flag still appeared in many sizes, with different star shapes and varying shades of blue and red. In 1912, President Taft set standard sizes and proportions that we still use today. The last change to the flag was in 1960. The fiftieth star was added for Hawaii, which had become a state the year before.

Conclusion

The long war was finally over. But in a sense, the American Revolution had just begun. Many challenges lay ahead for the new nation and its government.

White Americans were now free to rule themselves. How would they achieve both liberty and security? Could a balance be reached between the states and the national government? How would small states like Rhode Island, Delaware, and Maryland get along with large states like Massachusetts, New York, and Virginia? Would the country break up into several parts? How would the United States pay its debts and become prosperous? Could the United States take its place in the world and keep its independence?

Perhaps most importantly, would the new nation live up to its own ideals? On April 19, 1783, the date of the eighth anniversary of the battles of Lexington and Concord, George Washington congratulated the Continental Army. He told the troops they had protected "the rights of human nature."

In the Declaration of Independence, Americans said they believed that "all men are created equal" and entitled to "life, liberty, and the pursuit of happiness." But within the United States not everyone was equal, and large numbers of people had no liberty at all. Different Americans defined the great American ideals differently. Some slaveholders, for example, thought they had a "right" to own slaves. Other white Americans thought they should be free to take over lands that Native Americans had lived on for centuries. And there were all sorts of conflicts between people about what made a fair society. Americans would have much to do in the years ahead.

Glossary

alliance	An agreement between two or more people, groups, or countries to side together during a conflict. Countries or people with such an agreement become allies.
artillery	Large firearms and weapons that fire missiles; and a group of soldiers that uses these weapons.
assembly	A group of people gathered together. People elected to make laws in the colonies and, later, the states formed assemblies that were part of local governments.
authority	The power to make decisions and rules, or the people who have that power.
bond	A certificate promising repayment to a person who has lent money.
confederacy	An alliance of several groups that agree to act together and support each other.
congress	A meeting to discuss issues. "Continental Congress," the name given to the first meetings of delegates from the colonies, was shortened to "Congress" and eventually became the name of the United States legislature.
constitution	The basic plan and principles of a government.
customs	The office that controls what goes in and out of a country. It charges customs duties, or tariffs, on exports and imports, and these are collected by customs agents or officials.
delegate	The person chosen to represent others at a meeting or in making decisions.
draft	The first version of a document, such as the Declaration of Independence, or the act of writing that first version.
executive	The branch of government that enforces laws.
export	To send something abroad to sell or trade. An export is also the thing that is sent, such as tobacco or cotton.
fortifications	Structures built or made stronger to keep out enemies.
frontier	The edge of something known or settled. In North America, the frontier for white settlers moved as they themselves moved west onto new lands.
import	To bring goods into a country. An import is also the thing that is brought in, such as tea or cloth.

infantry	Soldiers who fight on foot.
legislature	The branch of government that makes laws.
Loyalists	People during the American Revolution who wanted the colonies to remain British.
mutinies	Actions in which soldiers refuse to obey orders.
outpost	A base in a foreign country or in an outlying area that is used for military defense or for trading.
Parliament	The legislature of Great Britain.
Patriots	People during the American Revolution who wanted the colonies to become independent.
peninsula	A piece of land jutting out from the mainland and with water nearly all around it.
policy	A plan or way of doing things that is decided on, and then used in managing situations, making decisions, or tackling problems.
repeal	To undo an earlier decision.
representation	Having someone to act on behalf of others: to give their views, look after their interests, and to vote for what they want.
resolution	A statement that declares the intention or opinion of an official group, such as a government body.
siege	A military operation in which attackers surround their targets and try to force them to surrender by bombarding them or cutting off their supplies.
Sons of Liberty	Organized groups of men in the American colonies who protested, sometimes violently, against British policies.
strategy	The overall military plan for dealing with an enemy or a conflict.
surveyor	A person whose job it is to measure land, work out boundaries and areas, and make records of the information.
treaty	An agreement reached between two or more groups or countries after discussion and negotiation.
trial by jury	A hearing before a judge at which a group of citizens decides whether someone is innocent or guilty of a crime.
writs of assistance	Documents of permission, issued by British courts, for officials to search Americans' warehouses, ships, stores, and homes.

Time Line

February 10, 1763	French and Indian War ends.
October 7, 1763	King George III issues Proclamation of 1763.
April 5, 1764	Parliament passes Sugar Act.
March 22, 1765	Parliament passes Stamp Act.
March 24, 1765	Quartering Act, passed in 1764, goes into effect.
October 7, 1765	Stamp Act Congress opens.
March 18, 1766	Parliament repeals Stamp Act and passes Declaratory Act.
June 29, 1767	Parliament passes Townshend Acts.
March 5, 1770	Boston Massacre.
May 10, 1773	Parliament passes Tea Act.
December 16, 1773	Boston Tea Party.
Spring 1774	Parliament passes Coercive (Intolerable) Acts.
September 5, 1774	First Continental Congress opens.
April 19, 1775	Fighting at Lexington and Concord.
May 10, 1775	Americans capture Fort Ticonderoga.
May 10, 1775	Second Continental Congress opens.
June 15, 1775	Congress appoints George Washington commander in chief of the Continental Army.
June 17, 1775	Battle of Bunker Hill.
August 1775– July 1776	American invasion of Canada fails.
March 17, 1776	British evacuate Boston.
January 1776	Thomas Paine's *Common Sense* published.
June 1776	British attack on Charleston fails.
July 2, 1776	Congress votes for American independence.
July 4, 1776	Congress approves Declaration of Independence.
August–September 1776	British drive Americans from New York City.
December 26, 1776	Battle of Trenton.
January 3, 1777	Battle of Princeton.
September 11, 1777	Battle of Brandywine.
September 26, 1777	British occupy Philadelphia.

October 4, 1777	Battle of Germantown.
October 17, 1777	General Burgoyne surrenders at Battle of Saratoga.
Winter 1777–78	Continental Army camps at Valley Forge.
February 6, 1778	United States and France make alliance.
June 1778	British leave Philadelphia.
June 28, 1778	Battle of Monmouth.
Summer 1778–Winter 1779	George Rogers Clark captures British posts in Northwest.
December 29, 1778	British capture Savannah.
July 1779	John Sullivan leads American army against Indians in Pennsylvania and New York.
September 23, 1779	John Paul Jones's ship *Bonhomme Richard* defeats *Serapis*.
May 12, 1780	British capture Charleston.
August 16, 1780	Battle of Camden.
September 1780	Benedict Arnold commits treason at West Point and joins the British.
October 6, 1780	Battle of Kings Mountain.
January 1781	Mutinies in Continental Army.
January 17, 1781	Battle of Cowpens.
March 15, 1781	Battle of Guilford Courthouse.
April–May 1781	Lord Cornwallis marches from North Carolina to Virginia.
March 1, 1781	Articles of Confederation go into effect.
October 1781	Siege of Yorktown.
October 19, 1781	Lord Cornwallis surrenders to Americans at Yorktown.
September 1782	Peace negotiations begin in Paris.
September 3, 1783	Treaty of Paris signed, ending war of American Revolution.
November 25, 1783	British pull out of New York City.
December 1783	George Washington resigns command of the Continental Army.
January 14, 1784	Congress ratifies Treaty of Paris.

Further Reading

Bober, Natalie S. *Abigail Adams: Witness to a Revolution*. Old Tappan, NJ: Simon and Schuster Children's, 1995.

Davis, Burke. *Black Heroes of the Revolution*. San Diego, CA: Harcourt Brace, 1992.

Devlin, Dean, et al. *Independence Day*. New York: HarperCollins, 1996.

Dolan, Edward F. *The American Revolution: How We Fought the War of Independence*. Brookfield, CT: Millbrook, 1995.

Ferrie, Richard. *The World Turned Upside Down: George Washington and the Battle of Yorktown*. New York: Holiday House, 1998.

Griffen, Adele. *Sons of Liberty*. New York: Hyperion Books for Children, 1997.

Martin, Joseph Plumb. *Yankee Doodle Boy: A Young Soldier's Adventures in the American Revolution Told by Himself*, ed. George F. Scheer. New York: Holiday House, 1995.

Santrey, Laurence. *George Washington: Young Leader*. Mahwah, NJ: Troll Communications, 1997.

Stratemyer, Edward. *The Minute Boys of Lexington*. Lake Wales, FL: Lost Classics Books, 1997.

Zeinert, Karen. *Those Remarkable Women of the American Revolution*. Brookfield, CT: Millbrook Press, 1996.

Websites

Lexington – The Battles of Lexington and Concord with commentary by individual participants and specifics about the battles.
russel.gresham.k12.or.us/Colonial_America/Lexington

Independence National Historical Park – Independence Hall and related historical buildings in Philadelphia.
www.nps.gov/inde/exindex.htm

Morristown National Historical Park Home Page – Preserves sites in the Morristown, NJ, area occupied by the Continental Army, 1777 and 1779-80.
www.nps.gov/morr/index.htm

Bibliography

Boatner, Mark M., III. *Encyclopedia of the American Revolution*. Bicentennial Edition. New York: McKay, 1976.

Bobrick, Benson. *Angel in the Whirlwind: The Triumph of the American Revolution*. New York: Simon & Schuster, 1997.

Cobb, Hubbard. *American Battlefields: A Complete Guide to the Historic Conflicts in Words, Maps, and Photos*. New York: Macmillan, 1995.

Commager, Henry Steele, and Richard B. Morris. *The Spirit of 'Seventy-Six: The Story of the American Revolution as Told by Participants*. Bicentennial Edition. New York: Harper & Row, 1975.

Fleming, Thomas. *Liberty! The American Revolution*. New York: Viking, 1997.

Keegan, John. *Fields of Battle: The Wars for North America*. New York: Knopf, 1995.

Middlekauf, Robert. *The Glorious Cause: The American Revolution, 1763-1789*. New York: Oxford University Press, 1982.

Morgan, Edmund S. *The Birth of the Republic, 1763–1789*. Chicago: University of Chicago Press, 1963.

Purcell, L. Edward. *Who Was Who in the American Revolution*. New York: Facts on File, 1993.

Smith, Page. *A New Age Now Begins: A People's History of the American Revolution*. New York: McGraw-Hill, 1976.

Index

Page numbers in *italics* indicate maps; numbers in **bold** indicate illustrations.